THINKERS
50

Innovation

Wake Tech. Libraries
9101 Fayetteville Road
Raleigh, North Carolina 27603-5696

Innovation

Breakthrough Thinking to Take
Your Business to the Next Level

STUART CRAINER + DES DEARLOVE

New York   Chicago   San Francisco   Athens   London   Madrid
Mexico City   Milan   New Delhi   Singapore   Sydney   Toronto

Copyright © 2014 by Stuart Crainer and Des Dearlove. All rights reserved. Printed in the United States of America. Except as permitted under the United States Copyright Act of 1976, no part of this publication may be reproduced or distributed in any form or by any means, or stored in a database or retrieval system, without the prior written permission of the publisher.

1 2 3 4 5 6 7 8 9 0   DOC/DOC   1 9 8 7 6 5 4 3

ISBN   978-0-07-182781-2
MHID   0-07-182781-1

e-ISBN 978-0-07-182782-9
e-MHID   0-07-182782-X

Library of Congress Cataloging-in-Publication Data

Crainer, Stuart.
  Thinkers50 innovation : breakthrough thinking to take your business to the next level / by Stuart Crainer and Des Dearlove.
     pages cm
  Includes index.
  ISBN 978-0-07-182781-2 (alk. paper) — ISBN 0-07-182781-1 (alk. paper)
  1. Technological innovations—Management. 2. Diffusion of innovations. 3. Creative ability in business. 4. New products. I. Dearlove, Des. II. Title.
  HD45.C686 2014
     658.4'063—dc23

                                                                    2013030616

McGraw-Hill Education books are available at special quantity discounts to use as premiums and sales promotions or for use in corporate training programs. To contact a representative, please visit the Contact Us pages at www.mhprofessional.com.

Contents

Introduction

After the Japanese company Fujitsu was acknowledged as having developed the world's fastest supercomputer, we spent time talking to those involved with its development.

The computer was nicknamed K, a play on the Japanese word *kei*, meaning the number 10 to the power of 16. It is a big number and a big project, with a $1 billion development budget and more than 1,000 people involved. Development began in 2007 and ended in 2012, with the K being celebrated as the fastest of the fastest.

We met with the managers and leaders who were involved in this huge project. We were struck by two things. The first was the down-to-earth nature of those involved. Those on the Fujitsu team were not classic Silicon Valley types. They were not hip or cool. There were no jeans, not even chinos. There was no casual wear, nothing casual at all. Indeed, when we met the overall project manager, he looked like a typical middle-aged Japanese corporate man wearing a suit with a waistcoat to stave off the Tokyo winter chill. These were ordinary people involved in an extraordinary project.

The second thing that struck us was that, despite their quiet and contained outward demeanor, these were men and women with a mission. We talked with Aiichirou Inoue, president of Fujitsu's Next Generation Technical Computing Unit. When we spoke, the project was nearing its end. The pressure was on. Inoue had been the driving force behind the company's mainframe computer business for 27 years. Given his long service, Inoue could perhaps have been forgiven for having an air of ennui. In reality, he was a ball of creative energy, excited and under pressure in equal measure. "In my previous roles, I couldn't do the things I wanted to do. I wanted to build something by myself, not just to use it, but to build it," he explained.

Talking to Inoue and his colleagues, it was clear that the innovative and groundbreaking K computer wasn't an end in itself. There were much more important and motivational forces at work. "I want the young engineers working on this project to be excited and to enjoy their work," said Inoue. "But, let's be clear: the K computer will make the future for Fujitsu, for Japan, and for human beings. It will give us the ability to look at the weather of the future, and there are a huge number of healthcare uses. That's what I mean about its power to change humanity. A computer is just a big box; what's interesting is to see it as a tool to help mankind and societies around the world."[1]

We walked away from the Fujitsu team and started thinking again about innovation. What we had encountered challenged our easily held stereotypes and assumptions. We learned that innovation is not practiced in isolation. Nor is it the work of supermen and superwomen, although much of what they accomplish is superbly world-changing.

Innovation is ordinary, but the results are extraordinary.

Innovation changes reality, but it is built from aspirations, dreams, ambitions, and visions.

We thought again, and this book combines our experiences of talking to practitioners in the field of innovation and the world's leading thinkers on the subject, including Clay Christensen, Vijay Govindarajan, Gary Hamel, Linda Hill, Costas Markides, Roger Martin, the late C. K. Prahalad, Don Tapscott, and many others. Our aim is to give you direct access to, and understanding of, the fundamentals of innovation and the latest thinking on the subject. Please let us know if we have succeeded.

Stuart Crainer and Des Dearlove
Thinkers50 Founders

How We Got Here

Innovation matters—now more than ever. Few managers would argue with the assertion that innovation is a business imperative. CEOs, academics, and politicians can be heard waxing lyrical about the need for innovation in this or that company, industry, or even national economy. But why does innovation matter so much in today's business world?

The answer is surprisingly simple. Innovation is where the worlds of business and creativity meet to create new value. It really is as simple as that.

The word *innovate* first appears in the mid-sixteenth century. It comes from the Latin *innovatus*, meaning "renewed, altered," from the verb *innovare*, which comes from *in* ("into") and *novare* ("make new"). In other words, innovation is all about finding new ways to change things. One useful definition of innovation is "the creation of new value."

What makes this all the more relevant today is that we live in a world where we are constantly demanding new value from the products and services we consume. Think about it. When did you last buy a new phone that boasted "the same old tried and tested technology," or a car that proclaimed itself "just as good as before"? Our ancestors might have been persuaded by claims of constancy and old-fashioned consistency, but today we demand more.

Blame it on fickle consumers, if you will. Or blame it on progress. But there is a continuous ramping up of our expectations, and this includes a heightening of our expectations of innovation. Companies are in the front line.

And it isn't just that the competition might add a new feature or button to an existing product. Commercial life can be positively Hobbesian: nasty, brutish, and, increasingly, short. Entire product categories can disappear overnight. Remember the VHS player? Remember the cassette recorder? Remember buying film for your camera?

One of the biggest challenges in dealing with innovation is dealing with *discontinuous innovation.* When technologies shift, new markets emerge, the regulatory rules of the game change, or someone introduces a new business model, many formerly successful organizations suddenly become vulnerable, and some of them are soon consigned to history.

A key part of the problem is that dealing with discontinuity requires a very different set of capabilities from what we are used to. Organizing and managing discontinuous innovation requires searching in unlikely places, building links to new partners, allocating resources to high-risk ventures, and exploring new ways of looking at the business. These are very different from the conventional and traditional approach to innovation. Historically, a company simply hired some very smart people, put them in an R&D lab, and let them get on with it. That approach is no longer sufficient.

One of the great challenges facing managers today is: How does an organization start building the capability for discontinuous innovation?

That is one of the questions that this book seeks to help you address. But let us start at the beginning. Obviously, innovation is as old as human life. In fact, some people would argue that the ability to innovate is the distinguishing feature of humanity and that it is what has allowed us to dominate the world in recent millennia—for better and for worse. (Let us hope, too, that it is also the redeeming feature that allows us to learn the lessons needed if we are to sustain our planet in the future.)

Along the way, there have been several leaps of innovation. We can point to the innovations that enabled our ancestors to move from being hunter-gatherers to farmers, for example, and later to develop agrarian economies. We can point to rich periods of experimentation and innovation in art and science that produced the Enlightenment and the Renaissance. All these are a testament to human creativity and inventiveness. But it is innovations in the commercial and organizational realms that are our focus.

Innovation and Business

There is a paradox here. The fact is, business and creativity are uncomfortable bedfellows. Indeed, *creative* is often a pejorative term in business—think of "creative accounting" or the broad-brush distrust of "creatives" in many organizations. The stereotypical corporate world is full of buttoned-up suits and left-brained rational decision makers, whereas the world we associate with creative endeavors is populated with undisciplined, scruffily clad, right-brained mavericks. It is the seeming disconnect between creativity and business that makes innovation so difficult for companies (especially large companies) to understand and manage. Yet, manage it they must because the need for innovation is becoming more and more vital to the success of all organizations.

The reason is simple: the world is moving ever faster. One by-product of this is that competitive advantage is increasingly fleeting. In today's turbulent and complex business environment, smart firms know that if they fail to innovate—both in terms of their products and services and in terms of their systems and processes—they will lose out to competitors. That's why they invest time and effort in creating systems, structures, and processes to ensure a sustained flow of innovation.

At the same time, the way we think about, understand, and execute innovation is being shaped by new ideas and fresh points of view from leading researchers, practitioners, academics, and management thinkers. Together with new innovation practices, the latest ideas and thinking about innovation are dramatically changing the innovation landscape. It should come as no surprise that the way we understand innovation itself is continuously being innovated!

This book captures some of the most significant ideas and perspectives that have transformed the innovation landscape in recent years, as well as those that will shape it in the coming years. As a result, it offers a lens through which we can understand an emerging set of ideas that will have—and are already having—a profound impact on the future of business.

Creative Destruction

So why is the impact of innovation so profound? To answer that question, you have to take a hard look at the capitalist system.

The Austrian American economist Joseph Schumpeter (1883–1950) coined the phrase "creative destruction." Today, it is almost as familiar as Adam Smith's "invisible hand" as an explanation of how capitalism works. And yet, how many times have you heard the phrase without considering the role of innovation in the capitalist mantra?

Innovation can be seen as the driving force behind Schumpeter's gale (as the forces of creative destruction are sometimes known). Taken as a whole, innovation is the animating wind of progress. If we break it down into the smaller storms of progress, then each new innovation can be seen as a small tornado.

There is nothing new in this. Far from the sun-kissed streets of California's entrepreneurial powerhouse in Silicon Valley, there was an earlier whirlwind that is much less appreciated today. The origins of the first explosion of commercial and industrial innovation occurred in Britain in the eighteenth and nineteenth centuries, during the Industrial Revolution. The winds of change it gave rise to blew around the world, having more influence in creating the British Empire than Britain's military might.

The Industrial Revolution was an outpouring of new ways of thinking and working as much as it was of sweat and blood.

Indeed, our modern sense of creativity, with its connotations of newness, originality, invention, and progress, was forged in the fire of commerce. (Ironically, during the Industrial Revolution, artists, rather than inventors, explorers, entrepreneurs, or industrialists, became the role models for creativity. But the industrialists kept the patent on innovation.)

Those same winds of creative destruction are still at work, constantly rampaging through the world economy. "Creativity and doing things differently are, if not identical, then nearly synonymous," says Jonothan Neelands, professor of creative education at the United Kingdom's Warwick Business School. "Doing things differently suggests a more creative approach to the world of business, but it is also a recognition that we cannot in any sphere of our lives continue as if we are not facing political, economic, social, and environmental crises that may engulf us. We are being battered by Schumpeter's now constant gale."

Time and time again, innovation unlocks the social and economic building blocks and reconfigures them for a new era. Throughout history, periods of social turmoil and change have been preceded by—or have given rise to—explosive bursts of innovation. Think of the Renaissance of the fourteenth century, the Age of Enlightenment in the eighteenth century, and the Industrial Revolution—or the current digital revolution, for that matter.

So, what do we know about innovation? Given that it is integral to the human condition, the answer is, surprisingly little. But there have been a handful of individuals whose track record suggests that they are worth listening to and learning from. One man with a genius for innovation was the American inventor and entrepreneur Thomas Alva Edison (1847–1931).

Sweat and Toil

"Genius is one percent inspiration and ninety-nine percent perspiration," Edison famously observed. This remains one of the most quoted—and insightful—observations ever made on the subject. It is testimony to his special place in the pantheon of innovation, too, that the lightbulb that he invented has become synonymous with new ideas and innovation. No examination of innovation could be complete without mentioning his precocious talent and his voracious appetite for fresh thinking.

To understand innovation, Edison's own life is instructive. His observation about the effort required to turn ideas into innovations was also the maxim by which he lived. By the end of his extraordinary career, Edison had accumulated 1,093 U.S. and 1,300 foreign patents. The inventor of the phonograph and the incandescent lightbulb also found time to start up or control 13 major companies. His endeavors directly or indirectly led to the creation of several well-known corporations, including General Electric and RCA. Consolidated Edison is still listed on the New York Stock Exchange.

Telegraphy was the catalyst for Edison's greatness. Edison was a natural with the Morse key, one of the fastest transcribers of his day. As a night-duty telegrapher, Edison was required to key the number six every hour to confirm that he was still manning the wire. Instead, he invented a machine that keyed the number for him automatically and spent his nights indulging himself at the local hostelries. Fired from a succession of jobs, he crossed the United States, working as a freelance telegrapher. Louisville, Memphis, Nashville, and Boston—Edison passed through them all before finally coming to rest in New York. He had by this time filed for his first patent—an automatic vote recorder for the Massachusetts Legislature.

It was in New York that Edison formed his first partnership with Frank L. Pope, a noted telegraphic engineer, to exploit their inventions. The partnership was subsequently absorbed by Gold & Stock, a company controlled by Marshall Lefferts, former president of the American Telegraph Company, who paid $20,000 to the two partners for the privilege. Recognizing Edison's ingenuity, Lefferts conducted a side deal with him, securing Edison's independent patents for the then princely sum of $30,000.

In 1870, with the benefit of some financial security, Edison hired Charles Batchelor, an English mathematician, and the Swiss machinist John Kruesi. He signed patent agreements with Gold & Stock and Western Union; took on a business partner, William Unger; moved into a four-story building on Ward Street in Newark, New Jersey; and started inventing on a grand scale. The fertile mix of minds at Ward Street quickly produced a stock printer, quadruplex telegraphy, and a machine to enable the rapid decoding of Morse.

The 1870s were the most creative period of Edison's life. Needing to expand his operation, he moved into buildings in Menlo Park, a town 24 miles from New York on the New York and Philadelphia Railroad. The name *Menlo Park* has become synonymous with innovation. It was there that Edison and his team perfected the phonograph. The patents were filed in December 1877, but Edison barely paused to draw breath; he began to experiment with incandescent filaments and glass bulbs. While he was still some way off from developing what would become the lightbulb, Edison managed to persuade a consortium that he could produce a commercially viable lighting system based on such a product. As a result, he signed a rights and remuneration agreement that laid the foundation for the Edison Electric Light Company.

In reality, Edison was far from developing such a product. Time passed, with Edison continuing to make favorable noises about progress, although he was actually making little headway in the lab. Feeling the pressure, at one point he retired to an under-stairs cupboard, took a dose of morphine, and slept for 36 hours.

It was on Wednesday, November 12, 1879, that Edison finally produced a bulb that remained lighted long enough to be considered of commercial value. It lasted for 40 hours and 20 minutes, and within two months, he had extended its longevity to 600 hours. Visitors trekked to Menlo Park to gaze in wonder at the lights that lit the roadway. Sadly, what followed for Edison was not the triumph of his invention but a period of protracted patent litigation that lasted more than 10 years.

The invention of the lightbulb and the formation of the Edison Electric Light Company marked the pinnacle of Edison's achievements. However, he did continue to invent. In the years that followed, a succession of new innovations emerged: DC generators, the first electric lighting system, electrical metering systems, alkaline storage batteries, cement manufacturing equipment, synchronized sound and moving pictures, and submarine detection by sound. His labs also threw off a slew of great minds, most notably Nikola Tesla, who was famed for his work on the Tesla coil and AC induction motors. The Wizard of Menlo Park, however, never quite recaptured the brilliance of his earlier years. Edison died on Sunday, October 18, 1931, working to the last.

Lessons in Innovating

So what are we to take from this remarkable innovator's life? Perhaps the greatest lesson of all about innovation: that a great idea leads to a genuine innovation only if it can be commercialized. Undoubtedly, a large part of Edison's genius lay in his realization that innovation alone was insufficient for commercial success. Edison focused on creating commercially viable products. To do so, he assembled a team of brilliant minds at Menlo Park. In effect, he created the first product research lab—a forerunner of facilities such as the celebrated Xerox PARC at Palo Alto, California. It was a practical and commercial approach to invention that proved to be immensely successful.

While it seems obvious that innovation without commercialization is a rather empty experience, it is worth noting that there are many, many innovations that fail to be commercialized or that are commercialized, but not by their creator. In their book *Fast Second*, Constantinos Markides and Paul Geroski developed this theme, pointing out that the originators of innovations as diverse as the jet engine, the typewriter, the pneumatic tire, and the magnetic tape recorder were not the people who eventually led these creations to mass commercialization. "The individuals or companies that create radically new markets are not necessarily the ones that scale them up into big mass markets," observed Markides and Geroski. "Indeed, the evidence shows that in the majority of cases, the early pioneers of radically new markets are almost never the ones that scale up and conquer those markets."[1]

Even with the caveat that innovation does not always lead to commercialization, innovation the Edison way provided the blueprint for the twentieth-century corporation. Innovation was neatly corralled under the umbrella of R&D. Groups of R&D technicians and scientists—geeks, we would call them today—worked on innovation and then passed the fruits of their labors on to the rest of the organization.

Tim Brown of the design company IDEO offers this take on Edison's contribution to our approach to innovation: "Edison wasn't a narrowly specialized scientist but a broad generalist with a shrewd business sense. In his Menlo Park, New Jersey, laboratory he surrounded himself with gifted tinkerers, improvisers, and experimenters. Indeed, he broke the mold of the 'lone genius inventor' by creating a team-based approach to innovation."[2]

Armed with the bright ideas that came out of the R&D lab, the company's job was then to commercialize the innovations on as large a scale as possible. At the time, this worked. Once a company had created an innovative product or service, it could build a large-scale operation to commercialize it. And it could build on a large scale, knowing that its advantage would last. For a large part of the twentieth century, a company that had a superior product or service could expect its advantage to last for years, even decades. Indeed, the primary purpose and rationale for large companies was to capitalize on their competitive advantage by leveraging economies of scale to drive costs down, and to defend their competitive advantage so that they could maintain a high price premium. The success of these large organizations was predicated not on their ability to innovate, but on their ability to earn higher profits through the efficiencies that flowed from economies of scale.

Mass production democratized many of the innovations that were being introduced, but it also had one unfortunate side effect: it made innovation more difficult. With scale came efficiency, but it also made it harder for companies to experiment and innovate.

Accelerating Change

As the twentieth century drew to a close, it was clear that the world was changing. As company after company in sector after sector has discovered, no competitive advantage is sustainable in the long run. If you have any doubt about this, ask the people who used to work at Kodak. A company that once enjoyed a seemingly unassailable position in the photography market was forced to file for bankruptcy in 2012 because it had failed to respond quickly enough to, and was eventually rendered redundant by, innovations in digital photography.

At its height in the 1980s, Kodak employed more than 60,000 people in Rochester, New York, alone. By the time it filed for bankruptcy in 2012, it employed fewer than 7,000 in the town, and it had closed 13 filmmaking factories and 130 photo labs around the world.

The collapse of the company's fortunes was dramatic. In the mid-1970s, it dominated the photographic market, accounting for 90 percent of all sales of film and 85 percent of the market for cameras. In the 1990s, new competition from the Japanese company Fuji Photo, which attacked Kodak from below with lower prices, ate into its market share. But it was the advent of digital photography that was its undoing. While Fuji and other rivals embraced the innovation, Kodak failed to respond quickly enough and found itself marginalized. By the time the company did react, it was too little too late. A similar story has been repeated in companies around the world.

The phenomenon of innovation as a commercial whirlwind that redraws entire industries is not new. What has changed is the speed with which new innovations routinely sweep away competitive advantage and reconfigure entire industries.

Witness what is happening in the global pharmaceuticals industry. In pharma, the traditional R&D model is firmly entrenched. Scientists innovate new combinations of molecules in their labs. These are turned into products and marketed. Now, however, competing companies have become more adept and much faster at developing and launching their own competing drugs. Indian companies such as Cipla, Dr. Reddy's Laboratories, Glenmark Generics, and Sun Pharmaceutical Industries have come from nowhere to become significant players in the global pharma industry.

The same thing is happening in other industries. In cell phones, Motorola first led the way; it was then displaced by Nokia, which had successfully reinvented itself; then came the BlackBerry, followed by the iPhone; and now Samsung is changing the marketplace once again.

In fashion, the Spanish company Zara has created its own brand of "fast fashion." It has the capacity to produce the latest fashions quickly at competitive prices. Its innovation lies in its process rather than its original designs.

As the face of innovation has changed, so, too, has the way we understand it and think about it. Today, experts talk about several different types of innovation:

- **Sustaining innovation.** A brand of innovation that occurs within an existing market, offering better value and allowing a company to compete with its rivals.

- **Efficiency innovation.** A type of innovation that reduces costs or increases productivity. Efficiency innovation was the driving force for much of the twentieth century.
- **Disruptive innovation.** A type of discontinuous innovation that has the power to disrupt existing markets and create new ones. Typically, disruptive innovation results from a new technology that replaces the incumbent technology.

Increasingly, innovation is being applied to processes and services as well as products. Today, innovations extend to everything from the use of biometric scanning to shorten the queues at airports to offering touchless credit cards to speed up financial transactions.

These and other changes are altering the innovation landscape.

Henry Chesbrough from the Haas School of Business at the University of California, Berkeley, and one of the world's leading innovation thinkers, puts this change into perspective:

> Vertical integration was the dominant business logic of the last century. Explained by Alfred Chandler and practised by General Motors, Standard Oil, DuPont and many others, it emphasized corporate centralization and integration. Underlying the logic was the belief that valuable knowledge was fundamentally scarce. As a result, companies sought to develop a knowledge advantage that others could not match.[3]

Chesbrough goes on to identify a number of working assumptions that accompanied this worldview:

- *The company that gets an innovation to market first will win.*
- *If you create the most and the best ideas in the industry, you will win.*
- *The smartest people in our field work for us.* Companies competed for the best and the brightest graduates and offered these recruits the best salaries and equipment.
- *If we discover it ourselves, we will get it to market first.* Internal R&D was seen as a barrier against smaller competitors.
- *To profit from R&D, we must discover it, develop it, and ship it ourselves.* The rise of companies like DuPont, General Electric, General Motors, IBM, Xerox, Merck, and Procter & Gamble was fueled by sustained investment in internal R&D. A by-product of this emphasis was the "Not Invented Here" syndrome, where companies rejected any technology that had come from outside.
- *We should control our intellectual property, so that our competitors don't profit from our ideas.*

The New Innovation Reality

We are now in a new environment where those assumptions no longer hold. The first characteristic of this new environment is the increasing emphasis on *disruptive innovation* (see Chapter 2). Every so often a whirlwind blows through an industry—usually caused by a new technology that is so radically different that it alters the shape of the industry completely and, in doing so, puts many existing, successful companies out of business.

For an organization to be truly successful and sustain that success over many years, it needs to be good at both types of steady-state innovation (sustaining and efficiency), and also to be able to sense when a disruptive innovation is on the horizon. This, though, is a notoriously hard juggling act and gives rise to what Harvard's Clay Christensen calls the *innovator's dilemma*.

The challenge for companies is that initially (when they first come to market), disruptive innovations are not attractive to an existing company's best customers, as they prefer the reliability and refinement of the existing technology. This causes a dilemma: should the company stick with its existing (often higher-margin) products, which its best customers want, or should it invest in a new technology that offers lower margins and will ultimately destroy its existing markets? For most companies, the answer is to stay with the existing technology. Unfortunately, this often means that the company is left behind and loses out when the new technology matures and replaces the incumbent technology. Hence, Kodak did not invest in digital photography until it was too late.

Being ready for discontinuous innovation requires a specific set of organizational skills, not least the ability to search for signs of a potential whirlwind that may sweep through an industry, or, as with the Internet, across entire business sectors around the world.

The second characteristic of the new innovation arena is *co-creation* (see Chapter 3). An idea championed by C. K. Prahalad, co-creation represents a profound shift in how new value is created, recognizing the increasingly symbiotic relationship between the firm and the consumer.

Related to co-creation, but spreading the innovation net still further, is *open innovation* (see Chapter 4). The phrase, coined by Henry Chesbrough, describes a radical new approach to innovation, exemplified by the open source movement that developed the Linux operating system. In recent years, open innovation has been embraced by some of the world's leading companies, including Procter & Gamble's Connect + Develop initiative.

The fourth emerging theme is *reverse innovation* (see Chapter 5). In the past, companies in the industrialized, predominantly Western, world came up with innovations and then exported them to the underdeveloped world. Reverse innovation turns this on its head, with products being developed in some of the world's poorest nations and then being exported to more industrialized nations.

The next major theme is *management innovation* (see Chapter 6). Gary Hamel and Julian Birkinshaw of London Business School are among those arguing most powerfully that how companies are managed offers the greatest potential for innovation of all. Indeed, Hamel believes that an entirely new take on management is required, what he labels Management 2.0.

A final and perennial issue is that of *leading innovation* (see Chapter 7). How best can a company's innovators be led and inspired?

These are the big ideas, but increasingly the battlefield has expanded. Some of the most interesting thinking and practice occur where *innovation meets strategy* (Chapter 8) and where *innovation meets society* (Chapter 9). The world is the stage for innovation, and now it is charged with tackling some of the world's most apparently intractable problems.

Disruptive
Innovation

Clay Christensen is an unlikely but compelling disruptive force in the field of innovation. Born in Salt Lake City, Christensen worked as a missionary for the Church of Jesus Christ of Latter-day Saints in the Republic of Korea from 1971 to 1973 and speaks fluent Korean. His career has straddled the worlds of academia and business. He worked as a consultant with the Boston Consulting Group (BCG) for four years and started three successful businesses, including CPS Technologies, a firm that he cofounded with several MIT professors in 1984.

Christensen became a faculty member at Harvard Business School in 1992 and was awarded a full professorship with tenure in 1998, becoming the first professor in the school's modern history to achieve tenure at such an accelerated pace. He is now the Kim B. Clark Professor of Business Administration and is widely regarded as one of the world's foremost experts on innovation and growth. In 2011, he was ranked number one in the Thinkers50.

In 2000, Christensen founded Innosight, a consulting firm that uses his theories of innovation to help companies create new growth businesses. In 2007, he founded Rose Park Advisors, a firm that identifies and invests in disruptive companies. Christensen is also the founder of Innosight Institute, a nonprofit think tank whose mission is to apply his theories to vexing societal problems such as healthcare and education.

The Ideas

Christensen is best known for his 1997 book *The Innovator's Dilemma: When New Technologies Cause Great Firms to Fail.* In it, he looked at why well-managed companies often struggle to deal with new radical innovation in their markets. These companies often fail, he suggests, because the very management practices that have allowed them to become industry leaders also make it extremely difficult for them to develop the disruptive technologies that will ultimately steal away their markets.

The idea of "disruptive technologies" was introduced by Christensen and Joseph Bower in a 1995 article in the *Harvard Business Review* entitled "Disruptive Technologies: Catching the Wave." Christensen and Bower noted that "one of the most consistent patterns in business is the failure of leading companies to stay at the top of their industries when technologies or markets change."[1]

Bower and Christensen pointed to a number of examples that were current at the time they were writing. For example, Goodyear and Firestone entered the radial tire market late, Sears gave way to Walmart, Xerox let Canon create the small copier market, and Bucyrus-Erie allowed Caterpillar and Deere to take over the mechanical excavator market. But the most striking example of this phenomenon is the computer industry.

IBM dominated the mainframe market but was slow to respond to the emergence of minicomputers, which were technologically much simpler than mainframes. Digital Equipment (remember it?) dominated the minicomputer market but in turn missed the personal computer (PC) market.

These observations led Christensen and Bower to pose the question: "Why is it that companies like these invest aggressively—and successfully—in the technologies necessary to retain their current customers but fail to make certain other technological investments that customers of the future will demand?"

In answering this question, Christensen and Bower argued that bureaucracy, arrogance, jaded executives, poor planning, and short-term investment horizons all play a part. But there is a more fundamental reason. Building on a model that Christensen had developed, he and Bower argued that there is a basic paradox at work—and it is that paradox that gives rise to the innovator's dilemma in the title of Christensen's 1997 book.

Too Close

At the heart of this paradox is the insight that "leading companies succumb to one of the most popular, and valuable, management dogmas. They stay close to their customers."

While received wisdom suggests that it is good management practice to listen to what your customers want, staying close to your customers can have an unfortunate side effect. In particular, listening to customers can mean that companies do not invest in or see the potential of new technologies that will ultimately disrupt their markets.

The reason for this is simple. When a new technology is first introduced, although it may be cheaper, it typically will not be as good as the existing—or incumbent—technology. This is not surprising, as the new technology has yet to be refined and perfected. At this stage, if the companies that supply the existing technology ask their customers whether they want the new technology, the answer will almost always be no. It is less reliable and less attractive.

Furthermore, the company is earning good margins on its existing technological innovations and has little incentive to invest in a new technology that will eventually compete with its existing products and earn lower margins. As a consequence, incumbent companies have no incentive to develop the new technology that will in time disrupt their markets.

Over time, however, the new technology is refined so that it offers many of the same benefits at a lower price. At this point, the customers who used to prefer the incumbent technology want the new technology and desert their former supplier. This, in essence, is the innovator's dilemma: Do you develop new technologies that your customers don't think they want and that will earn you lower profits? Or do you continue to invest in improving the products that your best customers love?

This dilemma is played out in industry after industry. What Christensen's model suggests is that the danger to an incumbent company usually comes when an inferior, cheaper product enters the bottom of the market. Over time, that cheaper technology evolves and moves up the value chain to displace the incumbent technology.

The computer industry is a good illustration of this process at work. Christensen's model has influenced the strategy of some of the biggest and most successful companies and leaders in the industry. When he was CEO of Intel, Andy Grove flew Christensen out to California to explain disruptive innovation to his top managers, then used it to craft a strategy to resist insurgent chipmakers. Christensen's influence is also cited as a major influence on Steve Jobs by his biographer, Walter Isaacson. Indeed, it can be argued that Apple's huge commercial success during Jobs's second stint at the helm is largely due to his success in resolving the innovator's dilemma.

And the effects of disruptive innovation are not confined to technological paradigm shifts. Disruptive innovation can take the form of new business models or new manufacturing processes.

So, for example, in the U.S. automotive industry, Ford and General Motors did not perceive the threat to their home market from Toyota's small cars. Instead of competing with the Japanese manufacturer, they preferred to concentrate on the more profitable midsize car and SUV segments. But over time, Toyota used its competitive advantage to move into these markets, and ultimately to attack the luxury car segment. Toyota now faces a similar incursion from Kia and other low-priced competitors.

So what can organizations do to safeguard themselves against disruptive innovation? Back in 1995, Christensen and Bower offered a method for spotting and cultivating disruptive technologies:

- Determine whether the technology is disruptive or sustaining.
- Define the strategic significance of the disruptive technology.
- Locate the initial market for the disruptive technology.
- Place responsibility for building a disruptive technology business in an independent organization.
- Keep the disruptive organization independent.

With his coauthors, Christensen has gone on to apply his model of disruptive innovation beyond business to include other sectors, such as education and healthcare. *Disrupting Class* (2008) and *The Innovative University* (2011) offer solutions for the education sector, and *The Innovator's Prescription* (2009) examines how to fix the U.S. healthcare system. Christensen's other books include *The Innovator's Solution* (2003), *Seeing What's Next* (2004), and *The Innovator's DNA* (2011).

Innovation Direct

Meeting Clay Christensen, the most disruptive element is his physical presence. He is an extraordinarily tall man with a daunting presence. In his office at Harvard Business School, we began by asking him this question:

> *What does it feel like to be recognized as the world's most influential management thinker?*
>
> I asked the same question of a friend of mine who is a professor at MIT. Broadly viewed, if they gave a Nobel Prize in Material Science, this guy would get

the first one. So I asked him the same question, and he said, "It is so disappointing to be judged as the best in the world because all my life I was at the bottom of the mountain looking up at the people at the top and thinking, man, they're smart. And now I'm sitting up at the top and thinking, well, if nobody's better or smarter than me, then the world is in real trouble! And so I'm very honored that people would think this of me, but the world is hurting!"

You follow in the footsteps of Peter Drucker, Michael Porter, and C. K. Prahalad, the other people who have topped the Thinkers50. It means that you are highly respected, but it also carries some responsibility as well.

Yes, and I am really honored. The obligation is that if there's anything I've learned about how to do research, I really have to teach the next generation to do much better research than I've ever accomplished. And if I can do that, then I feel like I will have accomplished something. If all I leave the world is a bunch of books, I won't have changed much.

Let's talk about those books. You're best known for the idea of disruptive innovation. What exactly is disruptive innovation? Explain it.

Disruptive innovation has a very specific meaning. It is not a breakthrough innovation that makes good products a lot better. It has a very specific definition, and that is that it transforms a product that historically was so expensive and complicated that only a few people with a lot of money and a lot of skill had access to it. A disruptive innovation makes the product so much more affordable and acceptable that a much larger population has access to it.

So a disruptive innovation involves the democratization of a technology?
That's exactly right. And so it creates new markets. But the technology leaders who made the complicated, expensive stuff find it very hard to move in the direction of affordable and simple because that is incompatible with their business model. And so it's almost a paradox within itself. But what it says is, if you're a little boy and you want to kill a giant, the way you do it is by going after this kind of product, where the leader is actually motivated to walk away from you rather than engage you.

Give us an example of this. Most people are familiar with the computer industry and how that's developed. Perhaps you can use that to illustrate the point.
Yes. At the beginning, the first manifestation of this digital technology was a mainframe computer. It cost several million dollars to buy, and it took years to be trained to operate these things, so that meant that only the largest corporations and the largest universities could have one. So if we had a problem that required this technology, we had to take our problem to the center and have the experts solve it for us.

But then there's a sequence of innovations from the mainframe to a mini to a desktop to a laptop and now to a smartphone that has democratized that technology to the point where everybody around the world has access to it and we are much better off. But it was very hard for the pioneers of the industry to catch these new waves. Most of those were created and dominated by new companies.

This process you describe gives rise to the innovator's dilemma, which was the title of your 1997 book. Can you explain that dilemma?
Yes. So the dilemma is that every day and every year in every company, people are going to senior management, knocking on the door, and saying, I've got a new product for us. And some of those entail making better products that you could sell for higher prices to your best customers.

But a disruptive innovation generally causes you to go after new markets, to reach people who aren't your customers, and the product that you want to sell them is something that is just so much more affordable and simpler that your current customers can't buy it. And so the choice that you have to make is, should we make better products that we can sell for better profits to our best customers? Or maybe we ought to make worse products that none of our customers would buy that would ruin our margins? What should we do? And that really is the dilemma.

It's the dilemma that General Motors and Ford faced when they tried to decide, should we go down and compete against Toyota, who came in at the bottom of their markets, or should we make even bigger SUVs for even bigger people? And now Toyota has the same problem. The Koreans, with Hyundai and Kia, have really won the low end of the market from Toyota, and it's not because Toyota's asleep at the switch. Why would it ever invest to defend the lowest-profit part of its market, which is the subcompacts, when it has the privilege of competing against Mercedes? And now Chery is coming from China, doing the same thing to the Koreans.

Your thinking has without question influenced generations of managers, including people like Steve Jobs and also Andy Grove at Intel.

Yes. I never imagined that I could ever meet these people, let alone be judged as having helped them. But I learned a lot from Andy Grove. What happened was that I was at Harvard Business School minding my own business, and Andy Grove called me out of the blue and said, "Look, I'm a busy man; I don't have time to read drivel from academics, but somebody told me you had this theory, and I wondered if you could come out and present what you've learned to me and my staff and then tell us how it applies to Intel."

And for me it was the chance of a lifetime, so I flew out there. Now, Andy Grove is quite a gruff man, and when I arrived, he said, "You know, stuff's happened to us; we have only 10 minutes for you, so just tell us what this theory of disruptive innovation means for Intel." And I said, "Andy, I can't do that because I have no opinion about Intel, but the theory has an opinion, and so I have to describe the theory."

So he sat back impatiently, and 10 minutes into it he stopped me and he said, "Look, I've got your stupid theory; tell us what it means for Intel." And he really did get it. And I said, "Andy, I need five more minutes because I've got to describe how this process of disruption worked its way through a totally different industry, just so that you can visualize what can happen to Intel."

So I described how the minimills came into the steel market at rebar and then went upmarket. When I was done with that, Grove said, "Oh, I get it. So what you're telling me it means for Intel is . . . ," and he described how Intel had two companies coming at it from below, and it needed to go down there and not let those companies go up against it from below. It was very successful.

And that was when Intel introduced its Celeron chip to counter cheaper competition from below?
Yes, that's right. And I thought about this. If I had been suckered into telling Andy Grove what he should do, I'd have been killed, because he knew so much more about microprocessors than I would ever know.

But rather than telling him what to think, I taught him how to think so that he could reach his own conclusions. And that changed the way I teach, it changed the way I talk, and the insight is that, for whatever reason, the way the world is designed, data are only available about the past. And when we teach people that they should be data-driven and fact-based and analytical as they look into the future, in many ways we are condemning them to take action when the game is over.

The only way you can look into the future is by using a good model. There are no data, so you have to have a good theory. And we don't think about it, but every time we take an action, it's predicated upon a theory. And so, by teaching managers to look into the future through the lens of the theory, you can actually see the future very clearly. I think that's what the theory of disruption has done.

And you've taken these ideas and applied them in nonbusiness areas—to healthcare and education. To what extent do you think that that's the role of management theory and management ideas? What has it got to offer in terms of solving the really big problems that the world faces?

It depends on the level at which you look at it. If you say, what does management have to offer to healthcare and education, I would say, not that much, because the techniques that are useful here may not be useful there. So to try to take lessons from the best practices here is a crapshoot, but if, in your research, you get to a fundamental level, the theories are broadly applicable. And therefore what we learn in the study of management, if we're figuring out what's the fundamental causal mechanism, really is broadly applicable.

Take motivation, for example. Motivation is in the face of every innovator in our school system. How do we motivate the students to get engaged? But it turns out that motivation isn't unique to education. It is in healthcare. How do we motivate people to take care of themselves? And in fact, in every business where you have a product and you're trying to convince the customers to be motivated to buy that product, it's the very same thing happening everywhere.

So if you understand the causal mechanism that leads people to pull something into their lives, then you don't have to become an expert in all these fields. Instead, you have the expertise in the problem. And I think that for me that's been really useful, because over the last 10 years we did two books, one in healthcare and one in how do we improve our schools, and we did them in parallel. And most people think, oh my gosh, you're an idiot; these are such different fields. But from my point of view, no, they're not such different fields; they all have the same problems.

And if you have theories that describe what happens at a fundamental level, you can do things like that and figure out that when you've solved this problem, where else you can use the same thing to solve the same problem?

Most recently, you've been applying some of this thinking or some of this thought process to your own life and asking how you will measure your life.

Yes. Again, this has just been a wonderful experience for me. I'll give you an example. We wrote a piece in the *Harvard Business Review* about the misapplied measures of financial analysis, and we pointed the finger at finance people because they have taught us some things that sometimes actually take you in a very bad direction, and one of them is this dogma that you should ignore sunk and fixed costs and look only at the marginal cost and the marginal revenue, assuming that what is sunk is sunk.

But that marginal analysis is very scary sometimes because what you have to be good at in the future is different from what you were good at in the past. If you look at the marginal cost of leveraging what is already in place versus the full cost of creating something completely new from scratch, the marginal argument always trumps the full-cost argument. And established companies just incrementally keep marginalizing on things that are irrelevant to the future.

And the same is true of people in their careers? So, people who come to Harvard Business School have a propensity to always want to be achieving something, and you've said that that marginal effect can be detrimental to their long-term aims?

That's right, because they look at the marginal benefit of just a little bit more investment in their career versus the cost of doing something else, such as throwing a ball with their kids. And because of the way they're doing the accounting, working late and investing a little more in their career looks very profitable. But by the time their children are in their teenage years, they look at it again, and they say, "Oh my gosh, I should've been investing in those kids all along, and now the full cost of reversing that problem is almost impossible to do." In the end, we pay the full cost, whether we know it or not.

CHAPTER 3

Co-creating
the Future

Innovation is still often associated with the lone creator working late at night in search of inspiration. If only innovation were that simple. Contemporary innovation is a team sport. Among the leading intellectual players in establishing this was Coimbatore Krishnarao Prahalad, better known as C. K. Prahalad. Prahalad (1941–2010) was the Paul and Ruth McCracken Distinguished University Professor of Corporate Strategy at the Ross School of Business at the University of Michigan. In the 2007 and 2009 Thinkers50, he was ranked number one—a position he retained until his untimely death in 2010.

Prahalad introduced the term *core competencies* to the management lexicon, and his bestselling book *Competing for the*

Future, written with Gary Hamel, set the strategy agenda for a generation of CEOs.

In 2004, Prahalad published two books: *The Future of Competition* (subtitled *Co-creating Unique Value with Customers*), written with Venkat Ramaswamy, introduced the notion of *co-creation*, while *The Fortune at the Bottom of the Pyramid* (with the ambitious subtitle *Eradicating Poverty Through Profits*) argued that the world's poor (the "bottom of the pyramid") represented an untapped market that was worth up to $13 trillion a year.

In *The Future of Competition*, Prahalad and Ramaswamy assert: "We are moving to a new form of value creation, where value is not created by the firm and exchanged with customers, but where value is co-created by the consumers and the company."[1]

Prahalad and Ramaswamy explained what they believed was a fundamental shift: "Business competition used to be a lot like traditional theater: On stage, the actors had clearly defined roles, and the customers paid for their tickets, sat back, and watched passively. In business, companies, distributors, and suppliers understood and adhered to their well-defined roles in a corporate relationship. Now the scene has changed, and business competition seems more like the experimental theater of the 1960s and 1970s; everyone and anyone can be part of the action."[2]

Relationships between companies and their suppliers and distributors were blurring, Prahalad and Ramaswamy argued, with the different groups sharing more information and collaborating on innovation. Walmart, for example, no longer simply distributes Procter & Gamble's products but also shares daily sales information, and the two companies collaborate to ensure efficient warehousing and replenishment of stocks. This was an example of how companies working together can co-create value.

To some extent, of course, companies have always cooperated with their business partners to introduce innovations. But the big change heralded by Prahalad and Ramaswamy was the growing importance of co-creation with customers.

The Grand Alliance

"The changing dynamics of business has been the focus of managerial debate the past few years. Practitioners and scholars talk about companies 'competing as a family.' They talk about alliances, networks, and collaboration among companies. But managers and researchers have largely ignored the consumer, the agent that is most dramatically transforming the industrial system as we know it," Prahalad and Ramaswamy note.[3]

It was the changing role of customers in the innovation process that co-creation championed. The active participation of customers in the creation of new products and services—enabled by the Internet in particular—is transforming how value is created and innovation occurs.

"The market has become a forum in which consumers play an active role in creating and competing for value," Prahalad and Ramaswamy observed. "The distinguishing feature of this new marketplace is that consumers become a new source of competence for the corporation. The competence that customers bring is a function of the knowledge and skills they possess, their willingness to learn and experiment, and their ability to engage in active dialogue."[4]

Prahalad, whose earlier work with Gary Hamel gave managers the language of core competencies, was now arguing that the ability to co-create and innovate with customers was the new competencies frontier. Companies that mastered co-creation would have a competitive advantage in the realm of innovation and customer satisfaction.

Some industries were further down the road than others in terms of developing these new competencies. The software industry, for example, has long sought to involve its customers in the innovation process, moving from testing new products in usability labs to testing them in customer environments. For example, millions of customers have tested beta versions of successive Microsoft Windows operating systems. These beta tests help the company identify and fix glitches in the early versions of the software and also help retain customer loyalty.

Other technology companies, such as Cisco Systems and some computer game developers, have gone even further, providing customers with open access to information, resources, and systems. Some game developers, for example, provide mapping and tools to allow customers to design their own battlefields and customize the look and feel of virtual characters.

So how can companies develop the competencies to co-create with their customers?

Prahalad and Ramaswamy identified four new imperatives:

- Encouraging active, explicit, and ongoing dialogue
- Mobilizing customer communities
- Managing customer diversity
- Co-creating personal experiences

Computer gaming companies like Blizzard Entertainment, the makers of World of Warcraft, routinely provide the tools to allow consumers to customize their characters and their environment. For example, the customer can choose whether he or she wishes to be an orc, a dwarf, a troll, or one of several different elven races, from night elf to blood elf.

These are all types of co-creation. But the idea extends far beyond the software industry. In particular, Prahalad saw an increasing role for consumers in shaping and creating their own value in areas such as healthcare. As he presciently observed:

> The availability of medical information on the internet and elsewhere is helping more and more patients enter into a dialog with their doctors. The more knowledgeable they become, the more likely these customers are to shape their healthcare regimen. Doctors may resent the consumer's exercise of his or her knowledge, but they would do well to learn how to co-opt it.

Prahalad was also prescient about the growing availability of personal data. He believed that, as customers and patients, we would soon be able to co-create a personal health profile with our healthcare providers. He believed that at some point, it would be possible for someone with diabetes, for example, to collaborate with a doctor and receive a personalized warning if his or her blood sugar had dropped to a dangerously low level. Such a co-created health innovation would save many lives.

New Age Thinking

In his final book, *The New Age of Innovation* (2008), coauthored with M. S. Krishnan, Prahalad took the notion of co-creation further, describing a new competitive landscape based on two simple principles: $N = 1$ and $R = G$.

We interviewed Prahalad on a number of occasions. He, too, saw these interactions as an opportunity for co-creation. At the end, he always turned to the camera operators and asked what they had thought of the interview. Their ideas mattered to him; their views were an opportunity for him to learn:

> *You grew up in India as one of nine children. What did those early experiences teach you?*
>
> Growing up in India is an extraordinary preparation for management. You grow up in large families, so you always have to make compromises; you have to learn to accommodate. And India is a very diverse culture in terms of languages, religions, and income levels, so you start coping with diversity at a very personal level as a child.
>
> The second point is that I was lucky because my parents were very academically oriented. My father was a judge and a great scholar. He told us very early in life, "There is only one thing that when you give more, you have more—and that's knowledge." That has stuck with me.
>
> Then, in the Union Carbide plant, I had to work with communist unions. I had to set rates—I was a young industrial engineer—and negotiating rates with the unions taught me a lot. They were very smart people, they were very thoughtful; and if you were fair and honest, you could deal with them in an interesting way. So it taught me not to think of these

groups as adversaries, but to collaborate, be honest, and be fair.

Running through your work is the idea of co-creation. Can you explain what it means?

Co-creation is an important idea. What it says is that we need two joint problem solvers, not a single problem solver. In the traditional industrial system, the firm was the center of the universe, but when you move to the new information age, consumers have the opportunity to engage in a dialogue and be active, and therefore, they can shape their own personal experiences. So, with co-creation, consumers can personalize their own experiences and the firm can benefit. And this is becoming much more common and possible today.

What would be an example of that?

Let's take Google; everybody Googles now. But if I look at Google, it does not tell me how to use the system. I can personalize my own page; I can create iGoogle. I decide what I want. Google is an experience platform. Google understands that it may have a hundred million consumers, but each one can do what he or she wants with its platform. That is an extreme case of personalized, co-created value. Our shorthand for that is "N = 1."

On the other hand, Google does not produce the content at all. The content comes from a large number of people around the world—institutions and individuals. Google aggregates it and makes it available to me. That is the spirit of co-creation, which says that even if you have a hundred million consumers, each consumer experience is different because it is co-created by that consumer and the organization, in this case Google. So resources are not contained within the firm, but accessed from a wide variety of institutions; therefore, resources are global. Our shorthand for that is "R = G," because resources are now coming from more than one institution.

So, N = 1 and R = G are going to be the pattern for the future.

How do these two principles apply to an organization, perhaps a large healthcare organization?
If you take what happens in a hospital, or what happens to me personally as someone who wants to maintain good health, each one of us is unique. We each have our own history of good health and health problems, so there are data about me personally. There is nothing that stops the doctors who treat me from taking me aside and discussing the risks and the benefits of following a certain regimen.

Can you give me an example of that?
Episodes of illness increase the cost of the healthcare system. So if you want to reduce the cost, you have to focus on wellness, and wellness requires the N = 1 approach. That's because we're all different and we

all have different propensities for disease—genetic and also lifestyle. So you have to get to that level.

For example, if people are a little bit obese, the doctor might alert them to the fact that they are susceptible to type 2 diabetes, that cardiovascular disease and high blood pressure are issues that they have to worry about. They can do that today.

So, for example, my doctor and I could look at my medical records and my episodes of illness and discuss a regimen to keep me healthy. That is a co-created regimen. The doctor cannot tell me to walk four miles every day because if I'm living near a run-down area, that may not be very wise. On the other hand, the doctor can make an arrangement for me to go to a gym so that I can exercise. Thus, I follow this regimen and the doctor keeps track of me.

How could you take that further?

Well, let us assume that I go to the next step; let us assume that I am a heart patient and I have a pacemaker. The doctor can say, all right, this is the bandwidth within which your pacemaker must operate, and, with your permission, we'll remotely monitor you. If something goes wrong, we'll send you a message, through a cell phone, through a PC, through the regular phone, or by sending somebody, telling you to get to the hospital because we need to treat you, or telling you to rest for two days. So the doctor can become my personal friend.

So that's the N = 1 part. What about R = G? How does that apply to a healthcare service?

Health is so important to all of us that it is critical that we get into an N = 1 way of thinking. We cannot continue to treat patients like they're an assembly line. But the R = G is more interesting. It says that the hospital can create an ecosystem where it doesn't do everything.

For example, I may have a social worker come and talk to me, or talk to women who are pregnant on what they should do to have a healthy baby. The hospital could have a relationship with an ambulance service, a relationship with a dietician, all kinds of relationships. For example, with type 2 diabetes, you can have testing labs that are not necessarily in the hospital. So as the patient I don't have to go and stand in a big queue.

So the hospital is part of a wider ecosystem?

Yes. The hospital can build a whole ecosystem of low-cost suppliers connected to the hospital, where the hospital becomes the nodal institution that sets the standards, that sets the parameters on how health security and privacy will be dealt with, and that also provides the system through which everybody gets paid for doing this. So the whole idea in healthcare is to help move away from treating illness to treating wellness and creating wellness. If you start from that perspective, then N = 1 and R = G become eminently possible—in fact, required.

What do these new ways of thinking about innovation mean for the way we lead? How do they change leadership?

I would say that there are three very important distinctions. First, leaders must lead. You cannot lead unless you're future-oriented. Leadership is about the future, it is about a point of view about that future, and it is about hope.

So that's the first point. And the other changes for leaders?

The second point about leadership is that it's not about the leader. The metaphor I like to use is that of a sheepdog, not a shepherd. A sheepdog has to respect some rules. Number one, you always lead from behind. Number two, you can bark a lot, but you don't bite. And, number three, you don't lose any sheep!

So, in other words, a leader is somebody who can bring out the best in you, not the best in him- or herself. That is a very different view. It's what Gandhi did. If you really think about Gandhi, looking at him, looking at his physical stature, looking at his clothes, nobody would have said that he would make a fundamental imprint on human history. But he was a great innovator—his leadership was about change; it was about hope; it was about freedom; it was a very personal thing. He made every Indian realize his or her own personal ability to contribute to that effort. And, very important, he set some nonnegotiables. It was not an armed struggle, it was a peaceful struggle, and that was nonnegotiable. So that would be my third principle: some things are nonnegotiable. Moral authority comes from having clear nonnegotiables. And that takes courage.

So for me, leadership is a point of view, the ability to mobilize people and make them achieve their very best and to have moral direction. It's not technological capability and economic strength; it's morality as well.

Innovation with Customers

There are two sources of co-creation that can compete for being the most overlooked: customers and employees. Increasingly, there is talk of the importance of improving employee engagement in order to harvest employees' bright ideas and creativity. On the customer front, there has been growing emphasis on the importance of the customer experience as a means of innovating with customers.

Among those championing a better understanding of customers as a route to innovation is Bernd Schmitt, the Robert D. Calkins Professor of International Business at Columbia Business School and author of *Big Think Strategy: How to Leverage Bold Ideas and Leave Small Thinking Behind* (2007). When we talked with Schmitt, we began by asking him about the customer experience.

How has the customer experience changed over the last decade?
It has improved. Retailing is entirely different from 10 years ago. Take a casual clothing line such as

Abercrombie & Fitch—the way it markets itself now in the retail space is entirely different. But it's not only about retailing. It's also about communications. It's about websites. So, the customer experience is a hot topic, and lots of companies are working on it. They're creating management positions within their organizations to create experiences for customers.

Is there one customer experience, or does it change with countries and cultures?

There's no doubt that there are cultural differences. An experience that might work in the United States may not work in Europe or Asia. So, you have to be very sensitive to customer trends, their needs and lifestyles, all of that. That's the exciting thing about customer experience management: you can never say, "We've fixed the experience now; this is how it is." You always need to update it; you always need to upgrade it.

Living in New York, I think it is natural to focus on the customer experience, because there are lots of interesting experiences around one, both in people's daily life and also commercially. When you look at the retail environment, for example, when you have contacts with the advertising agencies and the communications businesses, you can't help but think that marketing is not only about rational things and stressing product characteristics and product specifications, but also about having to be creative and unusual in the approach that you're using with your customers. New York is a great laboratory for studying what's going on with customers, but it's only one laboratory. That's why I travel a lot. Being a city person, I like to compare how companies market themselves in different parts of the world. There are many different industries, companies, and countries; so, without a doubt, there are many different kinds of customer experiences.

China is really improving a lot of customer experiences. Think about the Maglev, the high-speed train in Shanghai. It's mostly a Siemens product, but in Munich, in Germany, they never put it on the tracks. In Shanghai, they have done it! It's a great experience to be in the city within 10 minutes, and there are many other ways in which China is helping to improve what it feels like to be a customer. Recently, when I went to China, right after I went through customs, an illuminated rating scale asked me to rate the officer in terms of how satisfied I was with the experience. That is world-class customs service. So, there are lots of interesting things going on in China with respect to experience management.

If the customer experience has improved in the last decade, where's it going next?
I think the customer experience will change in several ways. First of all, customers are very concerned about going green and buying green products, and about companies being serious about being green. So, we will be seeing a lot of changes in this regard

from companies that are trying to win the hearts of consumers. I also believe (and this is a major change) that customers will want to be more casual and more connected—even emotionally connected—with companies. They don't want to do business with big, anonymous conglomerates that they don't know anything about and that may be behaving in unethical ways. So, I think we'll see a lot of more interactivity and openness in the transactions between companies and consumers.

So customers will come to expect more from companies. That's right, and that is a challenge for experience management. When expectations increase, companies have to live up to the new expectations, and that requires a new management style. Management needs to be constantly in touch with customers, understanding what they expect and responding accordingly. But this is something that will make companies better.

This all sounds like something that would be hard to teach in a classroom. Is it? I sometimes bring customers into the classroom. That's number one. Companies should be doing the same thing; they should bring customers into their organizations. Also, I teach my students a lot of the new technologies and the new research methods that are focused on customer insight—for example, methods that involve running focus groups not in a laboratory, which is an artificial environment, but in stores. So, we talk about research techniques in my class, and we practice them. And I sometimes take students into the field. We do a retail tour in New York City and watch what's going on—observing customers in their natural environments (something that I think companies should also be doing). I think these are great techniques for understanding customers and for understanding the customer experience. The classroom is a great starting point for learning about customers.

Some companies treat customers poorly. Do you have a sense of why they allow themselves to lag in this area?

I think what's holding them back is that many companies are still very bureaucratic. Sometimes they are afraid to interact with customers and perhaps discover that customers don't like the way they have been treated. I think that's the major reason: fear of the customer. Think about it. Customers can be very frightening because they can be very demanding. And you may not want to know about it. You think you have much more control if you are just staying inside the organization.

The customer experience is a major factor in any company's strategy, so, ignoring customers is shortsighted. All my work has been about creativity and doing new things. Customer experience is about innovation with respect to the customer. My book *Big Think Strategy* is, more broadly, about how to be innovative, how to develop an innovative, creative strategy within the organization. In the book, I give managers tools on how they can source bold ideas, turn them into a strategy, and launch that strategy.

What if managers are not just shortsighted, but stuck?
I remember going to a hairdresser in Hong Kong, and he asked me where I part my hair. I told him, "On the left." Then he asked how long I had been doing that. I said, "I don't know—40 or 45 years." And then he said, "You won't for the next 40." This was a great inspiration for me. What he was doing at that moment was, in a way, killing a sacred cow: that I had parted my hair on the left and never thought of doing it any other way. And in companies you have lots of these sacred cows, things that they have always done in a certain way. And they therefore believe that these things must be done that way. Everyone makes certain assumptions that are never questioned—managers, too. It can be very enlightening for a company to make a list of those sacred cows and then come up with alternatives to the ways that things are done. In such a process, many managers come to realize that there are often no good reasons for doing a lot of things the way they have always been done.

Have you tried this exercise with managers?
When I do workshops with organizations, managers can easily come up with a list of 20 or 30 sacred cows involving how with the company deals with

operations, marketing, and new product launches. They come up with these sacred cows, and then they develop alternative ways of managing such important tasks. Not all of those alternatives will be a great improvement on the way things are done at present. The alternative ideas have to go through an evaluation process, and so on, but this is one way of sourcing bold ideas. The exercise usually pays off with many new ideas that can be implemented.

Are companies structured to think big?

Most companies are extremely conservative. They are also very bureaucratic. They are usually organized in silos that don't talk to one another. When you do a big think strategy, you need to break through that; you need to break down the silos. And you need to have procedures and tools on how to source bold ideas, such as looking outside the business. A technique that I use a lot in my workshops is to ask managers to perform outside-industry benchmarking. Many companies benchmark within their industry— airlines look at other airlines—but they also need to get ideas from the best performers in other industries and what they're doing.

All of this requires bold leadership, does it not?

I'm very interested in leadership these days. The notion of leadership as something analytical—about decision making in a status quo situation in which one chooses the best possible option—is only one particular part of leadership. Another part of leadership is to look into the future, to be creative, to create new worlds. For that, companies need different leadership skills.

Can you help them learn new leadership skills?

The companies I work with hire me to help them to grow, to see the world in new ways, to imagine new realities. Most businesses have a leadership team with some conservative, status quo–oriented managers working along with those who really want to revamp their business. Of course, if the business is in a dynamic industry, then the company has no choice but to think outside its current operational and strategic box. Either way, developing a big think strategy can be helpful.

Opening Up Innovation

Innovation was once safely corralled in the R&D department and kept in creative quarantine. And there it largely stayed throughout the twentieth century.

In the new century, this has been fundamentally changed. The change has been ignited by three realizations. First, pumping more money into R&D does not necessarily lead to more or better innovation—as many companies have discovered to their cost.

The challenges of R&D are well illustrated by the pharmaceutical industry. The pharma giants spend millions on drug development. The Tufts Center for the Study of Drug Development, for example, estimates that the development costs for each drug hitting the market are a staggering $802 million.

But despite the massive amounts of money that are being spent, drug approvals have fallen in recent years. The drug pipeline is beginning to dry up.

If pharma companies, which have traditionally been some of the most innovative organizations, are struggling to make money from their R&D investments, maybe conventional innovation models are no longer valid. The closed model of innovation, with in-house R&D conducted in secrecy and profit earned on patented products, may have had its day.

The second realization was that a company's innovators are uniquely powerful. The inventor of a new drug or the developer of a bestselling computer game can bankroll an organization for years. Such people need to be handled with care. As organizations have come to realize the importance of this small coterie of smart individuals, they have sought out better ways to manage and lead them.

In parallel, there has been another realization: that a company does not have a monopoly on great ideas. Over the last decade, we have seen company after company broaden the reach of its innovation activities in an attempt to access ideas from customers, suppliers, employees, and interested bystanders.

Opening P&G

Take the story of Procter & Gamble, which we looked at with Julian Birkinshaw of London Business School, where he launched the Management Innovation Lab.[1] In 2000, P&G was at a crucial point in its long history. One of the world's best-known corporations and the creator of some of the world's most famous and successful brands was at a crossroads. Its CEO, Dirk Jager, had left after a mere 18 months in the job. In March, the company announced that it would not meet its projected first-quarter earnings. The stock price was spiraling downward, falling from $116 per share in January to $60 by March. The massive loss of $85 billion in market capitalization was matched by the loss of confidence within the company. It provoked a media frenzy. Perhaps most poignantly, *Ad Age* headlined its front-page story: "Does P&G Still Matter?" It was one of many column-inches devoted to the company's apparently impending demise.

P&G's then new CEO, A. G. Lafley, provided an instant dose of reality:

> We weren't delivering on goals and commitments to analysts and investors. Major P&G businesses were underperforming—only three of them accounted for 80 percent of the total value created in the 1990s. Competitors were swooping in and gobbling up market share. We were overinvested: we overbuilt capacity, hired too many people, funded too many aggressive introductions of new products and expansions of existing brands. P&G brands were not delivering good consumer value: we weren't consistently leading innovation, and prices were too high. We had priced up big, established brands to pay for new products and aggressive geographic expansion. Our costs were also too high. We had frayed relations with important customers, who were frustrated with incompatible strategies, poor service levels, and P&G's inability to create value for them. We were too internally focused. Consumed with the massive reorganization, and with

so many people in new jobs, we were all spending too
much time managing internal transactions.

In addition to this litany of internal problems, P&G had
the abiding corporate challenge of achieving growth. A mature
company such as P&G is usually expected to deliver organic
growth rates of around 4 to 6 percent every year. Historically,
this growth had been delivered by the company's formidable
research and development resources—thousands of researchers
spread worldwide. But with the proliferation of new technologies and intensifying competition, P&G's standard approach to
R&D was under threat. Only 35 percent of its new products met
their financial objectives. R&D productivity was stagnant.

Lafley's prescription for the ailing corporate patient was
wide-reaching. Estimating that it would take three years to get
P&G back on track, he focused the company on four core businesses (accounting for 54 percent of sales and 60 percent of
profits); its big, established leading brands; and P&G's top 10
countries (80 percent of sales and 95 percent of profits). Costs,
which had skyrocketed under Jager, were cut. Capital spending, which had leapt to 8 percent of sales, was trimmed. Nearly
10,000 jobs were lost around the world as underperforming businesses were closed and the company left businesses that were
now regarded as nonstrategic. Some product lines were discon-
tinued, investments were written off, and brands such as Comet,
Crisco, and Jif were sold off.

And, perhaps most boldly of all, in the midst of establishing the new P&G order, Lafley announced an entirely new
approach to innovation. P&G's corporate innovation fund had
increased sevenfold in four years. Two-thirds of these projects

were cut. Lafley announced that in the future, instead of relying on its internal research and development, P&G expected that 50 percent of its innovation would come from outside the company. The R&D numbers would remain the same, but the focus would be on maximizing ideas both internally and externally.

The logic was simple. For every one of the company's researchers, P&G calculated that there were 200 people—scientists or engineers—outside the company who had talents that the company could utilize. Instead of thinking in terms of having 7,500 people in corporate R&D, P&G recalculated that there were 1.5 million people worldwide whose knowledge the company needed to tap into. Research and development was reincarnated as Connect + Develop with an organization of 1,507,500 people.

Reality and Development

The positioning of Connect + Develop was important. First, it was made clear that Connect + Develop was not about outsourcing P&G's research and development capability. It was about finding good ideas and bringing them in to enhance and capitalize on the company's internal capabilities. In essence, it was an insourcing strategy. The second point was that Connect + Develop was not billed as a "transformation" program.

It focused on three areas: the needs of consumers (each business and the company as a whole identified the top 10 consumer needs), adjacencies (products or services that could help P&G capitalize on existing brand equity), and what the company labels "technology game boards" (a planning tool that enables P&G to evaluate how technologies in one area affect other areas of the business).

At the heart of Connect + Develop is using networks to gain connections to new ideas. In the old invention model, "know-how" was key, and this was what companies really focused on the most. In the new connections model, "know who" became critical. The networks that P&G keys into are varied. Among the most notable are proprietary networks developed specifically for Connect + Develop. For example, P&G's leading 15 suppliers have around 50,000 people employed in R&D. P&G built an IT platform to share technology briefs with suppliers. Closer working relationships and the sharing of information brought a 30 percent increase in projects with staff from suppliers and P&G working together.

Even competitors were seen as sources of inspiration. P&G also created a network of what it calls "technology entrepreneurs." The technology entrepreneurs number 70 worldwide. They are effectively the eyes and ears of Connect + Develop, making contacts within industry and education, with suppliers, and with local markets. The technology entrepreneurs have brought more than 10,000 products, ideas, and technologies to P&G's attention. Each is then evaluated.

The Innovation Dividend

The result was that P&G accomplished its goal. More than 50 percent of the company's innovations now originate outside the company. When A. G. Lafley first announced his bold target in 2000, the figure was under 15 percent. Connect + Develop has helped turbocharge more than 250 products into the marketplace and generated billions of dollars in sales.

Opening up innovation is increasingly necessary and popular.

Open innovation, powerfully championed by Henry Chesbrough, executive director at the Center for Open Innovation, part of the Institute for Business Innovation at the Haas School of Business, offers an alternative model.

It was pioneered by the open source software movement, which championed a more open attitude toward innovation, turning the notion of intellectual property on its head by publishing its computer source code on the Internet for anyone to see. The open source movement even allowed programmers to take the code and modify it, contributing to the final product. The result was, in many people's eyes (not least the consumers'), a better product. The Linux operating system, the Firefox web browser, and the Thunderbird e-mail client are all extremely functional open-source software products.

Says Chesbrough: "We have moved from closed innovation to a new logic of innovation: *open innovation*. This new logic builds upon the recognition that useful knowledge is widely distributed across society, in organizations of all sizes and purposes, including nonprofits, universities, and government entities. Rather than reinvent the wheel, the new logic employs the wheel to move forward faster."[2]

It is a case, as Chesbrough points out, of companies realizing that "not all the smart people work for us." As he notes, "Their realization is that, in a world of abundant knowledge, hoarding technology is a self-limiting strategy. No organization, even the largest, can afford any longer to ignore the tremendous external pools of knowledge that exist."[3]

Spreading Innovation Wings

Today, companies in all sectors are being urged to embrace the collaborative principles of open innovation. In their 2002 article in *Harvard Business Review*, "Open-Market Innovation," Darrell Rigby and Chris Zook identified several benefits associated with open innovation: more ideas are generated and a broader base of expertise is accessed, leading to improvements in the "cost, quality, and speed" of innovation; licensing new innovations to third parties may provide a needed stimulus within the organization to make more use of internally generated ideas; and exported ideas may receive more intense scrutiny and so a more rigorous test of the economic viability of the idea.

Open innovation has spread beyond the open source movement into many different sectors. In the electronic consumer goods market, for example, many of the leading players realize that it is not possible to keep pace with consumers' insatiable appetite for new products without adopting a more open innovation model.

The net gainers are companies like Quanta Computer in Taiwan and Wipro in India. Companies like these are known as original-design manufacturers (ODMs). They design and assemble electronic equipment for the major brand names like Dell and Sony. And, where once they might have built to design specs supplied by the client, increasingly they are driving the design innovation.

Such outsourcing of R&D is not without risk. Motorola used an ODM, BenQ Corporation in Taiwan, to design and build mobile phones. BenQ subsequently moved into the China mobile phone market, selling its own branded products. There is also investor sentiment. When a company has outsourced just about everything, including the innovation, what is left of proprietary value other than the brand?

Open Today

Most companies, no matter how progressive, may take some time to adopt a completely open approach to innovation. Indeed, they may never do this. Ensuring a fair exchange of value between innovation partners is still a challenge. There are real risks involved in open innovation, alliances, joint ventures, and partnering arrangements that simply do not exist in licensing and in-house R&D. Not the least of these risks are unwanted technology transfer and spillover, and lengthy, costly legal disputes. Until firms find ways of managing these and other risks, new innovation models may remain just a great idea rather a business reality.

However, while there is some risk, there is also a huge upside in terms of competitive advantage through innovation. Many commentators and industry practitioners were convinced that innovation was one thing that couldn't be outsourced. Various arguments were put forward, from the need to stay close to the customer to the risk of giving away intellectual property. The innovation outsourcing revolution that is currently underway suggests that the doubters were wrong.

"Open innovation is a paradigm that assumes that firms can and should use external ideas as well as internal ideas, and internal and external paths to market, as the firms look to advance their technology," Chesbrough explained in his 2003 book *Open Innovation: The New Imperative for Creating and Profiting from Technology.*

In 2006, Chesbrough wrote *Open Business Models: How to Thrive in the New Innovative Landscape*, which examines how companies may innovate the ways they create and capture value from their businesses. More recently, Chesbrough has turned his attention to the world of services with his 2011 book *Open Services Innovation: Rethinking Your Business to Grow and Compete in a New Era.* In it, Chesbrough explains how companies can, with the help of open innovation, make the shift from product-centric to service-centric thinking.

As Chesbrough explains: "Over the past two decades things have fundamentally changed. It is still true that no company can grow and prosper without new ideas. It is also clear that the changing needs of customers, increasing competitive pressure, and the evolving abilities of suppliers necessitate continual creative thinking for a company to stay ahead of the pack. The challenge is that the distribution of this critical knowledge has shifted. This has important implications for how every company thinks about growth and innovation."[4]

Open to a Point

But this is not to argue that all industries have migrated or will migrate to open innovation.

For example, the nuclear-reactor industry depends mainly on internal ideas and has low labor mobility, little venture capital, few (and weak) start-ups, and relatively little research being conducted at universities. Whether this industry will ever migrate toward open innovation is questionable.

At the other extreme, some industries have been open for some time now. Consider Hollywood, which for decades has innovated through a network of partnerships and alliances among production studios, directors, talent agencies, actors, scriptwriters, independent producers, and specialized subcontractors such as the suppliers of special effects. And the mobility of this workforce is legendary: every waitress is a budding actress; every parking lot attendant has a screenplay he is working on.

Many industries, including copiers, computers, disk drives, semiconductors, telecommunications equipment, pharmaceuticals, biotechnology, and even military weapons and communications systems are currently undergoing a transition from closed to open. For such businesses, a number of critically important innovations have emerged from seemingly unlikely sources. Indeed, the locus of innovation in these industries has migrated away from the confines of the central R&D laboratories of the largest companies and is now situated in various start-ups, universities, research consortia, and other outsiders. And the trend goes well beyond high technology. Industries such as automotive, healthcare, banking, insurance, and consumer packaged goods have also been leaning toward open innovation.

Their realization is that, in a world of abundant knowledge, hoarding technology is a self-limiting strategy. No organization, even the largest, can afford any longer to ignore the tremendous external pools of knowledge that exist.

The Science of Serendipity

At the heart of open innovation is open-mindedness, or being willing to accept ideas from elsewhere in whatever form they arrive and at whatever time.

The reality remains that the vast majority of innovation occurs inside large companies—often in the face of stifling bureaucracy. Matt Kingdon, the cofounder of the innovation consulting firm ?What If!, argues that it is corporate innovators battling within large, established organizations who are the real heroes of innovation.

Kingdon has spent the past 20 years on the front lines of innovation, bringing new products and services to market and helping organizations, including the likes of Unilever, PepsiCo, Google, and Virgin Atlantic, become more innovative.

In particular, Kingdon argues that the phenomenon of serendipity—seemingly happy accidents that occur during an innovation—is less random than we might think. By gaining a better understanding of the patterns by which serendipity occurs, large organizations can increase their chances of these sorts of happy accidents taking place.

At Pfizer, for example, the discovery of Viagra was in no small part helped by the fact that the researchers' offices were, in their own words, "old and dilapidated"; they were crammed into a small space, with the entire team of chemists and biologists bumping into one another all the time. This close, seemingly random proximity helped the flow of information and the cross-pollination of projects and thinking. It was via a corridor conversation between two scientists working on very different projects that one of the scientists learned of a breakthrough in another field that led to the development of Viagra.

According to Kingdon, companies that deliberately foster serendipitous cultures and environments are more likely to hit the innovation jackpot. "Serendipitous invention and the creative exploitation of ideas is a muscle that you can choose to work out or allow to wither," he says.

In *The Science of Serendipity*, Kingdon dissects the ways in which corporations are designed to support or obstruct innovation. He traces the dilemmas that executives in a wide variety of firms face, and details the steps taken to overcome the issues and get great ideas across the goal line.

The book identifies and examines five key factors. First, it looks at the sort of person who is good at serendipity, arguing that the best people to lead innovation initiatives have respect for the organization but do not revere it so much that they cannot bend the rules.

Second, people who are good at innovation deliberately seek out new stimuli to provoke their thinking. Third, they are adept at making ideas as real as possible quickly, using rough models and prototypes to give ideas concrete expression. The fourth factor in fostering serendipitous innovation is designing a physical environment that forces people who are working on different projects onto a collision course that causes them to bump into one another and cross-pollinate their thinking. Finally, Kingdon offers advice on how to deal with organizational politics, which can so easily derail innovation.

His advice on battling the corporate machine? "It's part of organizational life, so get over it and get on with it!"

The Science of Serendipity *is a great title for a book, but wer're guessing that you're using the word* science *fairly loosely.*
Well, yes. Anyone who knows me, knows I'm not a scientist. I'm a storyteller, really, and I just got very interested in this concept of serendipity. Number one, it's a lovely word to say. It rolls off the tongue

in a very mellifluous way. But the more I looked into the word *serendipity*, the more subtle it became and the more questions it threw up, and the more linkage there was between serendipity and the reality of how innovation happens in large organizations. If you think about it, when you talk to somebody in a large organization about how a great new innovation has actually happened, when you peel back the layers of the story, what you don't find is a load of clever people sitting around a boardroom table strategizing their way to the end. It just doesn't happen like that. It's much more a story about people who bump into each other, who have random chance meetings or seemingly chance meetings. Their head is in the right space. They have the right attitude. They're asking the right questions. They say things like, "Let's work on a Saturday," or, "What do you mean by that?" They're not shooting people down. They're not cutting people off. It's a combination of the right people, right place, right attitude, and right behavior; that's the real story of innovation.

One of the greatest examples of serendipity, or how an organization was wired to make itself more likely to be lucky, which is the real meaning of serendipity, is the very fascinating story of the invention of Viagra. We all know what Viagra does, and it's well known that the little blue pill was given to 12 chaps in Cardiff in Wales for an angina trial. And when they came in on the Monday morning, they said, with big grins on their faces, "We're not giving you the pills back!" So the researcher called the surprising results back to base at Pfizer's headquarters.

In those days, Pfizer's research people were located in a town called Sandwich in Kent. And they were in fairly ramshackle buildings where people were scrunched in together, and several people were able to overhear the results. They were then able to contribute to the results. It was a mishmash, what we might call today a mash-up or the original hack-athon of people contributing ideas from diverse scientific backgrounds. Together they pieced the story together and realized that what they had discovered was something that could increase Pfizer's company value massively so that it could buy Lipitor [the cholesterol-lowering statin that became the bestselling drug in pharmaceutical history, with sales of $125 billion]. And, briefly, Pfizer became one of the most valuable companies in the world in terms of market capitalization.

It's an amazing story. How do you get a company so big and so powerful created almost through a chance discovery? The reality was that it wasn't quite as much chance as you might think. There was some thinking that went into the culture beforehand.

The subtitle of the book is How to Unlock the Promise of Innovation in Large Organizations. *And, of course, that's a bigger challenge, isn't it? Because it's all very well for youngsters starting a new company to take risks and do innovation. It's much harder in big organizations. Can you say a little bit about that?*

I've found over the years that if you talk to somebody in a large organization about an entrepreneur—we all know the names of some famous entrepreneurs in Silicon Valley, or whatever—the snore factor's pretty loud. And people start to roll their eyes up to heaven because we all know that when you're young and you've got nothing, then taking a risk is fun. Now, when you get a bit older, like me, and let's say you're working in a large corporation, and you've got a family, you've got dependents, you've got a job, you've got a career ahead of you, then risk tastes very different from what it does to, say, a 20-year-old wearing a cool black turtleneck sweater in Silicon Valley. So I think the real heroes of innovation are the people in large organizations who have all the stress and strain that we all know so well that come with an organization that, let's face it, makes its money through repeating itself, maybe doing things a little bit better. But these are the real heroes of innovation. How can they make things happen in a big organization?

And the way you describe it, there are five elements to this. Let's take them one by one. The first is all about the sort of person who drives innovation in a large organization.

I call the first section the Protagonist. This is the lead player in the play of innovation in a large organization. There is a characteristic of somebody in a large organization who can make innovation happen. These people respect the organization they work for, but they don't revere it. And this is really, really important. I describe them as having a "captain one minute, pirate the next" mentality. And this is an important little phrase because one minute they're standing on the prow of a ship, like a captain: we're going that way. The next minute, you might find that same person down in the bowels of the boat fixing the engine, using a bit of old tubing and not going by the instruction manual. It's that sense of knowing the big picture of where they're going or what they want to try to do that powers innovators in large organizations, that gives them the license to act a little bit more like a pirate.

And the second element?

The second lesson I've called the Quest for Innovation. What you find with large organizations is a very simple equation, and that is that the intelligence that they feed themselves can very often be very similar to the intelligence that their competitors are feeding themselves. So it is the same sorts of researchers talking to the same consumers and talking to them in the same way. And you'll find that a lot of great innovation breakthroughs come from asking yourself a really basic question, which is, how can I look under stones that my competitors aren't looking under? How can I be sure that my intelligence is competitive, is new?

So we followed some corporate innovators to find out what type of customers they interact with, where they go, how they talk to people, and where they get their stimulus. And one of the things we found, for instance, is that a lot of innovation is born out of angry people. It's born at the margins. Let's face it, if you're in a big business, you don't really want to leave your office to hang out with people who are angry and don't like your business very much, but actually those are the very people you should be listening hard to.

And the third element is what we might know as prototyping?
The third element I've called Making It Real—and I've deliberately not called it prototyping or iteration or experimentation. These are very well-known concepts, particularly in the digital world, where access to customers is very cheap and you can change your offer very quickly. We have a belief at ?What If!, which has been honed over 20 years, that one of the most important things you can say in the world of innovation is, how real can I make it now? And it's the now bit that's really important.

And what we found is that, whether you're discussing a new concept for a hotel or a new type of automobile, there are always ways in which you can make your concept a little bit more real. Maybe you can draw it; maybe you can act out the service delivery; maybe you can quickly run the numbers on something. But in the history of innovation, what separates the really successful people from the others is that they make lots of little trials of their product. And in a big company, the easiest way for us to do that is to ask ourselves the question, how real can we make this now?

And the fourth element is something you alluded to earlier. It's about the environment, creating a fertile environment for innovation.

Yes, the fourth element of *The Science of Serendipity* is a hobbyhorse of mine. I call it Collision Course, but it's really about the environment we're in. We all know that somehow the space around us is really important, but we don't really know why. A lot of offices these days, where a lot of people work, may have a groovy reception area. But once you go upstairs, there's quite a lot of cubicles, quite a lot of silence. They have meeting rooms that are designed to be functional; they're not particularly inspirational a lot of the time. And organizations that are good at helping people bump into each other are good at helping to mix up a diverse group of ideas, so they use the space to create ideas.

A great example would be Pixar's offices in Emeryville, California, where they have several thousand people in one building, and they have two bathrooms. But everyone needs to pee and everyone needs to eat, and if you can get people to mash up during the day so they're bumping into each other, then you're more likely to combine ideas. Previously you would have had to call a meeting or schedule a meeting or rely on someone organizing that in advance.

And finally, of course, we have the realpolitik of innovation, the politics that happens in any organization. Can you say a little bit about that?

The fifth element of *The Science of Serendipity* I've called Battling the Corporate Machine. And this is the really, really practical part. I've never worked in a large organization, or worked with a large organization, where there is no resistance to change. It just doesn't happen. So what I say to innovators is, it's a bit like when you split with your first girlfriend or boyfriend: sometimes the greatest advice is, get over it. Move on. There will always be resistance to innovation in large organizations. Live with it. But how you present the numbers, how you present the ideas, how you win over the naysayers, how you share the excitement from some of the insights that underpin a great idea—these are all things that can be planned in advance. And people who win at innovating in big organizations think through the voyage of an idea through an organization and plan for the battle ahead.

Senior executives often say that we mustn't be afraid to fail, but you don't see too many people who fail getting promoted. So how do you take risks in an organization where there is a real fear of failure?

It's a funny thing, fear of failure in a large organization. If you talk to senior people in an organization, they often say that they want the people underneath them to take more risks. If you talk to the people underneath them, they talk about their bosses and say the bosses won't let them take more risks. I think there's something going on that is holding people back, and the answer to it is to lower the stakes. Take many more risks, but take much smaller risks, things that you can do maybe under the radar, things that are easy to do by Friday, rather than things that you can only do over the next few months and that require huge capital expenditures.

The number one thing is, how can we reduce the stakes around here? I think the number two thing is bearing in mind that the grapevine is one of the most powerful ways of making something happen or killing something in an organization. Now, the grapevine in a company, the gossip structure, needs feeding with stories of innovation success.

So, it's about taking a small risk, getting something to happen, and telling the story about what happened, so that your innovation drive can gather credibility. You can make things happen because people see things happening. They see the output, the impact of what you're doing. So, smaller risks and stories, these are the two things that are within the control of people at whatever level in an organization. And you'll find that people at a very senior level in an organization very much like telling stories about some of the troops who have maybe stepped a little bit out of line, and maybe done the right thing for the company. They've respected the company, but they haven't necessarily revered it. They've made something happen. There is a huge hunger within an organization for stories about people who are making a difference—the unsung heroes, if you like.

Most companies have loads of data on how their customers behave. How helpful is that in really understanding what customers want, and what else could managers do to uncover unmet customer needs?

It's true that most companies have loads of data on their customers, but this is the problem: they have too much data. They are drowning in data. They have so much data that they don't really feel what customers feel. And to be an innovator, you have to go out on a limb. Think about it. You have to do something that isn't easy. You have to really know that it's the right thing to do. You have to be really motivated. The way to get motivated in a large organization is generally to hang out with a customer who's got a problem or who's got a vision for how things could be better in the world, and to be in that customer's home, or with his family, or wherever he is when he makes the decision to purchase. Try to get as close to that moment of purchase and consumption, as close as possible to the problem that the customer has in the world.

And, once you've seen that, to an extent it becomes your mission, your rallying cry: this is what

I'm going to change. Now, that's data as well, but it's not data that you'll find on a spreadsheet or that's given to you thirdhand by a market researcher. That's experiential, feeling information, and that is the most important thing that innovators need in a large organization.

In most organizations, there is a received wisdom that says, this is how our industry works; this is what our customers want. That can make it hard to get people to accept a new idea. How do you convince people that that wisdom is wrong and that your idea is worth pursuing?

People at work aren't bad. Most people at work—in fact, almost everybody I've met—are good-hearted. They have good intentions when it comes to furthering their company, wanting their peers and their colleagues to succeed. But we are so busy at work that when someone comes at us with a new idea about how things could be improved—almost never a finished idea, probably a bit of a scruffy idea—it's sometimes a pain in the ass. Frankly, too much creativity is a pain in the ass.

So the more people at work can demonstrate how an idea might be taken through the system, the more they can make it real. Rather than say, "I've got a rough idea about something," the more they can say, "I had an idea; I drew it; I showed it to my wife and my kids; they made these comments; do you want to take a look?" All of a sudden this isn't just enthusiastic but slightly mad ramblings from a colleague.

All of a sudden this is something that has just a little bit more credibility, a bit more of a hook. So I think the way to move things through an organization is to make those things as real as possible.

CHAPTER 5

Back to the Future

The playing field for innovation has widened. Executives throughout the world are sweeping up the latest inspirations and insights from increasingly diverse sources—from sports; from the arts; from the sciences. Inspiration knows no boundaries.

This was brought home to us when we met one of the best chefs in London, the Cinnamon Club CEO and executive chef, Vivek Singh. The Cinnamon Club is situated near the Palace of Westminster in a building that was previously Westminster Public Library. Singh has been the culinary driving force behind the Cinnamon brand since it was launched.

Singh reinvented Indian cuisine, offering a range of groundbreaking dishes that used the best ingredients available in London in traditional Indian recipes. Once the restaurant was a success, Singh could have paused for breath and enjoyed the plaudits. Instead, he decided to change the menu every day. The bar was raised.

"One of the older guys that I'd hired locally came to me and said, 'Chef, it's none of my business, but with all due respect, you've got to be careful with what you're doing. You're putting everything out; one day you'll run out of ideas, and then there'll be no value. And they'll get rid of you. You're young, you're enthusiastic, I totally respect all of that, but you don't need to change menus every day,'" Singh told us.

He thought differently. "Actually, the more you create, the more ideas you have. Whenever we meet, we often talk about it, and he says, 'You were right. By creating new dishes, you never run out of ideas; you come up with more new ones.' And I think that's what we found, and our team finds as well. The challenge now is to meet expectations. Today, commercial success is also on the agenda as part of those expectations. We are constantly innovating, never standing still."

There is a restless energy to Vivek Singh. The next challenge can't come quickly enough. Anyone who spends hours in steaming kitchens tends to need energy to burn. Singh is a restless improver and tinkerer. Dishes are chopped and changed, and never revived. "If you leave something on the menu too long, people get comfortable with it. And once they get comfortable with it and start recognizing it, they won't try other things and experiment," Singh said. "For us, it's so important we change; change is the thing that is a constant on our menus. No matter how successful you are, you always become a victim of your own success; therefore, we need to accommodate change."

Indeed, the most popular dishes are clinically eliminated. At the end of every year, the most successful dish is taken off the menu and replaced. The change, he explained, ensures that comfort zones never become permanent. "The dishes that sell the most can be overrated, in the sense that they might account for 40 percent of sales. So, at the Cinnamon Club, that would mean that 40,000 people are having one dish. After a while, no matter how passionate the chef is, fatigue will set in, so that the excitement, love, and passion clearly aren't there."

Change keeps the chefs fresh. At the other end, Singh is equally counterintuitive and loath to change dishes simply because they aren't selling. "If it doesn't sell, it says something about the people who are coming in, or it says something about the people who are selling it. So if it doesn't sell at all, it means that either my staff isn't able to explain the dish, or people aren't adventurous enough."

The Other Side of Innovation

Keeping the cuisine theme, we shared innovation ideas with Vijay Govindarajan, known as VG, at one of his favorite restaurants.

Govindarajan, the Earl C. Daum 1924 Professor of International Business at the Tuck School of Business at Dartmouth College, received the 2011 Thinkers50 Breakthrough Idea Award for his idea for designing a $300 house.

Govindarajan has published nine books, including the international bestsellers *Ten Rules for Strategic Innovators*, *The Other Side of Innovation*, and *Reverse Innovation*.

Fundamentally, Govindarajan argues, organizations are built for efficiency and not for innovation.

*Why do you say that organizations are built for
efficiency and not for innovation?*

One side of innovation is coming up with ideas; the
other side of innovation is execution, so that's where
I got the importance of the topic.

Take a look at a company like the New York
Times Company. For 150 years, it has excelled in the
newspaper business. In that business, it is all about
efficiency. In the mid-1990s, the managers said,
"There is something called the Internet, and we'd
better reinvent ourselves on the Internet." Therefore,
the company created New York Times Digital, which
was its way to create an innovative business model
on the web. That is all about innovation, whereas
the core business is all about efficiency. How do you
maintain two conflicting paradigms inside the same
company? That's the real challenge.

And they are, fundamentally, conflicting?

The core business, the *New York Times* printed newspaper business, is all about being repeatable and
predictable. The more you can make every activity
repeatable and predictable, the more efficient you can
be. Innovation is exactly the opposite; it is about the
nonroutine and the unpredictable. That's the conflict.

*Shouldn't big organizations simply give up on inno-
vation? They can outsource it and bring it in from
elsewhere.*

That is the Schumpeter kind of argument, which is creative destruction, with one company being destroyed by another. My problem with that premise is if a company doesn't innovate, it's going to die because every business model has only a finite life. As a result, the company life cycle will be similar to the business model life cycle, and we don't want that to happen.

How do you define innovation in this sphere?
Innovation to me is adapting to change, and, again going back to the publishing example, one of the big changes was the Internet, which is a technology change that you have to adapt to. That's what innovation is all about.

What are the principles that allow large organizations to really deliver on innovation?
I think the principles are very easy. There are three of them. However, even though they are easy to say, they are difficult to do.

Principle number one: if you want innovation, you have to create a dedicated team that is separate from the core.

Principle number two: the dedicated team, while separate, cannot be isolated. It needs to work in partnership with the performance engine of the company, its core competencies.

The third principle is that innovation, by definition, is an experiment, and experiments have unknown outcomes; therefore, don't judge the innovation team based on its results, judge it based on its ability to learn.

The first principle sounds a bit like a skunkworks, which is an old idea. How is what you're suggesting different?
It is not a skunkworks because a skunkworks says, "Let's send the innovation team to the basement, far away from the core business," whereas what we're saying is that innovation has to be an activity that's a partnership between a dedicated team and the performance engine. Therefore, you cannot isolate the innovators. They have to work in close collaboration with the core business.

The performance engine is something that you talk about a lot. What do you mean by that?
The performance engine is your core business because every organization has an established business. The established business is the foundation, and you never want the foundation to crack. So the performance engine has to really sustain excellence because innovation is only an experiment for the future, whereas the performance engine is the foundation for the present, and that's what throws off the cash that you can invest in innovation.

What's the role of leadership in this?
Leadership is terribly important because when we say that innovation is a partnership between a dedicated team and the performance engine, the leader

has to make sure that this partnership is healthy, since there are natural points of conflict. The performance engine is all about routine and predictability; the dedicated team is all about being nonroutine and unpredictable. So, if you're trying to make these two things work together, there are going to be conflicts.

One way to avoid conflicts is to keep the two groups separate—that's the skunkworks approach—but that loses the advantage of the established business. So keeping them together and managing them creatively, that's the role of the leader.

What were the results of the research that really astonished you?

There was one big surprise for us. When we started the research, we thought we would need different execution frameworks for different types of innovation. There are incremental product innovations; there are radical product innovations; there are sustaining innovations; there are business model innovations; there are all kinds of innovations. So we thought execution would be different for the different types, but what we found is that the three principles that I laid down really apply across the board. One playbook is good enough to implement any type of innovation.

Are you optimistic that multinationals will learn the lessons you outline?

Without question, because repeatedly, when we talk to companies, they say that their biggest struggle is in execution. There are two types of execution. There is day-to-day execution, which is what the performance engine does, then there is innovation execution. These are completely different disciplines, and companies are very good at day-to-day execution. What they really lacked was a framework, a set of ideas and insights, for innovation execution.

Hasn't the teaching at business schools contributed to the situation where organizations are focused on efficiency and not on innovation?
I think this whole notion of innovation is a relatively new phenomenon, a new emphasis. Even management, as a discipline, is a relatively new phenomenon. When we started in the mid-1970s, the concept of strategy was that, as described by Michael Porter's five forces framework, strategy is stability. His idea was that you should find a position inside your industry and then erect entry barriers to protect that position. It was only in the mid-1990s that we said that strategy is instability: it is about really creating change; it is about really innovating. Therefore, this notion of strategic innovation is only about 15 years old, so the study of its execution is even more recent.

The entire area of execution is interesting because it is what managers pride themselves on, but you're saying that they're quite blinkered.
When they say that they focus on execution and that they're good at it, they're talking about being good at

day-to-day execution. Innovation execution, in fact, is fundamentally different. The day-to-day execution methodology will kill innovation, so they know one half of the equation; what we are telling them is that there is the other half of the equation.

One of the problems with innovation is, how do you teach it?

Innovation has two components, as I said. One side of innovation is ideas, creativity. Perhaps that is difficult to teach, since creativity may well be something that is an art, something that you are born with, although there are some people who say that you can also structure the process, so that you can become more creative. But the bulk of innovation is commercializing creativity, and commercializing creativity can be taught because there is a disciplined process by which you can take an idea and make it into a big business. Therefore, that part actually can be taught. Innovation can be taught.

There's an irony in that the roots of some of the great corporations of today are in innovation. Car companies, for instance, were innovators at the beginning of the twentieth century, but they've lost contact with innovation, presumably.

In fact, this is an irony with any company because when you are a start-up, the only way you can succeed is by being innovative. If you don't have an innovative idea, you're going to die. The companies that are born will become successful only if they're innovative. What they forget is that they need to continue the process because if you stop innovating at any point, you're going to die. So in some sense, you're right in saying that we need to go back to the foundation and say, "What is it that we had at that time that made us so innovative, and how can we keep that spirit or bring that spirit back?"

The more cynical would say that actually, innovation is probably overrated and that the companies that succeed often are not the most innovative, but the second company to get to the market—for instance, Amazon. This is an argument that Costas Markides of London Business School has made, that the companies that are second to market can be the most successful.

The way I would answer that is this: the way I define innovation is adapting to change. It is quite possible that someone went first and made a lot of mistakes, and you are learning from those mistakes; therefore, you are able to commercialize or take that idea and make it successful. Our focus is not on whether you're first or second; our focus says that whether you're first or second, the execution challenge remains the same.

Wisdom in Reverse

In 2008, Govindarajan took a leave of absence from Tuck to join General Electric (GE) for 24 months as the company's first professor in residence and chief innovation consultant.

At GE, Govindarajan's role was threefold: to teach, guide, and consult with GE managers on their innovation practices and key projects. Govindarajan also worked with Jeff Immelt, GE's CEO, to produce the *Harvard Business Review* article "How GE Is Disrupting Itself" (September 2009).

The article, written with Immelt and long-term collaborator Chris Trimble, introduced the concept of *reverse innovation*—where, contrary to conventional expectations, innovation takes place in emerging markets and then is brought back into developed countries. Reverse innovation was rated by the *Harvard Business Review* as one of the big ideas of the decade. The book *Reverse Innovation* (with Chris Trimble) was published in 2012.

When we talked to Vijay Govindarajan, we began by asking him about the concept of reverse innovation.

How do you explain the concept of reverse innovation?
If you think back historically, global companies innovated in their home markets, which are the developed world, and took the products they invented into the developing countries. Reverse innovation is just doing the opposite; you are innovating in the emerging markets and then bringing those innovations back into developed markets.

So it's the opposite of glocalization, which is a dreadful word, but which was the big idea of the 1990s?
Yes, without question. And the reason that glocalization worked historically is that in the 1980s and 1990s, American companies were taking their products into Europe and Japan, where the customers

were similar to U.S. customers. But that does not work in emerging markets because the whole market structure and the customers' problems are so fundamentally different.

Just look at GDP per capita. In India, it's $800. In the United States, it is $50,000. Therefore, there is no product that you make in the United States, where the mass market per capita income is $50,000, that you can adapt and sell in India, where the mass market per capita income is $800.

Can you give me an example from GE of reverse innovation at work?

Take, for instance, the ultrasound machine. In the United States, an ultrasound machine looks like an appliance. It's huge, it's bulky, it costs anywhere from $100,000 to $350,000, and it can carry out very complicated applications.

Now consider the situation in India; 60 percent of the population lives in rural areas where there are no hospitals, so patients can't go to the hospital. In large parts of India, the hospital has to come to the patient. That means that you can't use those bulky machines. The machine has to be portable. Again, what customers can afford is different. So what GE did was to create a portable, low-cost ultrasound machine that costs somewhere in the neighborhood of $15,000, which is a fraction of the cost of the bulky machines that GE sells in the United States, and that has opened up a huge market in China and India.

And that same portable ultrasound machine is now coming into the United States and creating new applications. This is a great example of reverse innovation.

Until moderately recently, wasn't India only 1 percent of GE's markets?

That is very typical of most multinationals because they sold the U.S. products in countries like India and China. That means that they were capturing 1 percent of the opportunity in those countries, and therefore those countries represented only 1 percent of their global revenues. But going forward, those emerging markets are going to represent a huge growth opportunity. In fact, I'd say that in the next 25 years, the biggest growth opportunity for multinationals is going to be customers moving from rich countries to poor countries.

And this changes the focus of innovation from research and development institutes in America, for instance, to creating innovations in India, on the ground?

Without question the biggest change for American multinationals or European multinationals is to shift their center of gravity to where the next innovation will take place. That means it is an organizational challenge. You have to put the resources where the opportunities are. That means you have to localize product development. You have to localize sourcing. You have to localize strategic marketing capability. This is probably the biggest mindset issue for multinationals.

So how long has GE been practicing reverse innovation?

It's a relatively new concept. I would say it has really caught on within the last five years, the reason being that this big nonlinear shift in which customers are shifting from rich countries to poor countries is a phenomenon that has occurred over the last five years. India and China opened up their borders in the last 15 years, but it's really only been in the last five years that we've seen the big, massive middle class emerging in these countries.

Reverse innovation sounds like a sensible idea. What are the blockers of it in large organizations?

Probably the biggest problem in having reverse innovation work in large companies is their historical success. We've talked about glocalization, which is taking a global product and selling it with some adaptation in local markets, but glocalization requires a fundamentally different organizational architecture. Thus, the more you succeed in glocalization, the more you're going to find it difficult to do a good job at reverse innovation. That's probably the biggest bottleneck: the historical success.

And did GE encounter those bottlenecks and problems along the way?

Without question. As a case in point, there was an executive in India—Raja is his name—who was head of GE Healthcare in India. Five years ago, under the glocalization model, his main responsibility was to distribute global products. And if he had to come up with a new concept to solve Indian consumers' healthcare problems, first of all, he would have had to do it during the weekend, because during the weekdays he was busy selling global products. But even if he had written up the proposal during the weekend, he then would have had to sell the idea to the global product head, who was sitting in Milwaukee. He had probably never visited India, and he didn't understand the problems of rural India. And even if Raja could have convinced him, there were a whole lot of other people he would have needed to convince. So it was a huge organizational challenge.

And there's a huge cultural challenge as well because for the guy sitting in Milwaukee, it doesn't sound like good news for him. But it sounds like good news for the people in India because it makes their jobs more interesting and the opportunity is greater.
I think you've touched upon the key issue here; it is a cultural transformation, and it has to change at the top. And Jeff Immelt, to his credit, visits India and China, and he encourages the CEOs of various businesses to visit these countries.

When Jeff Immelt sits with the premier of China and talks to him about what the key national priorities are, he gets firsthand information about the possibilities in China. Or when he meets with the CEOs of Indian companies, he begins to understand what it takes to win in India. That kind of firsthand understanding on the part of the CEO is the starting point for bringing about this cultural shift.

So it really changes the job for American and European leaders in businesses like GE? They've got a different role now?

They have got a different role, and it is really about creating a new global mindset. I think only companies that have leaders with a global mindset will be able to win in this new era, where the opportunity has shifted from developed markets to developing markets.

You see, historically, 15 years ago, global companies used to think of their global strategy in terms of the strategy for Europe, the United States, Japan, and the rest of the world. Today, and going forward, they have to think about their global strategy in terms of their strategy for the BRIC countries, the Middle East, Africa, and the rest of the world—and the rest of the world includes the United States, Europe, and Japan. That's the mindset shift.

And do you think American executives have that global mindset? Famously, only 25 percent of Americans actually have passports.

I think this is probably going to be the most significant challenge for American multinationals. They have a lot of talent, but do they have talent with the global mindset? That is the question. So I say, the biggest challenge for American multinational CEOs is to say, how can they embed that mindset?

Thinking of previous CEOs of GE, Reg Jones, in the 1970s, became known for portfolio planning, and Jack Welch became known for Six Sigma and a lot of other things. What do you think Jeff Immelt will go down in history for?

One of the interesting things about GE is that when the CEO changes, it is not for demographic reasons: the CEO has become old, so you replace him with another CEO. It is because the company wants to effect change. In fact, every CEO puts a new strategic frame on the company, not because the old frame was irrelevant, but because it's a new environment; it's a new world.

And the strategic frame that Jeff Immelt is putting on is, without losing the performance discipline that Jack Welch put in place, how do you add the innovation discipline? And Jeff Immelt's legacy will be judged by how well he is able to incorporate innovation within a company that is known for efficiency.

GE seems very good at disrupting itself if there's no room for complacency, and that's really been true for the last 100 years, hasn't it?

Without doubt. I think that is one of the remarkable things about General Electric. It's a company that's more than a hundred years old, and the only way you can survive that long is if you make yourself obsolete in terms of products and solutions. And this is the real hallmark of GE: that it's willing to change; it's willing to embrace new ways of competing.

What surprised you about GE? You haven't worked so closely with a big corporation before, have you?
What really surprised me is that I never thought that one person could have such an important impact, particularly in a large company like GE with more than 300,000 employees. And what I've found was, amazingly, that as an outsider, I did have some strengths that an insider did not have. I didn't have a big title there, I didn't have a big budget, and I was not running a big business, but because I was coming in as an academic, my viewpoint was unbiased.

CHAPTER 6

Innovating Management

Management does not stand still. The way managers manage in the second decade of the twenty-first century is already substantially different from the way they managed at the end of the last century. Even so, a powerful call for revolution rather than evolution has filled the managerial air in recent years.

Leading the calls to the managerial barricades are Julian Birkinshaw of London Business School and Gary Hamel, best known as the coauthor of *Competing for the Future*. They have focused on the importance of *management innovation*, a company's ability to effect fundamental changes in its own internal way of working. Looking into the performance of exceptional organizations, Birkinshaw and Hamel identified management innovation as a crucial but largely overlooked factor. As they say:

Consider GE's rise to iconic status in the early years of the twentieth century. This was driven by its creation of the world's first modern R&D Lab. By bringing management discipline to the chaotic process of scientific discovery, GE was able to bring more new products to market more effectively than any of its early competitors. To take a contemporary example, think of Toyota's long and uninterrupted reign as the best volume car manufacturer in the world. This massive achievement owes much to Toyota's success in harnessing the problem-solving skills of all of its employees as to technological mastery.

Management innovation lies at the heart of both GE's and Toyota's success. Innovating the way things were done in both these organizations—and many others we discovered—was key to securing competitive advantage. Additionally, it was notable that the advantage achieved through management innovation was very difficult—sometimes impossible—for competitors to copy.[1]

Birkinshaw and Hamel's research, under the auspices of the Management Innovation Lab that they formed, found that there are several vital ingredients that always come together when management innovation happens:

- A distinctive and novel point of view on the future
- A clearly articulated problem or challenge that needs resolving

- A core group of heretical thinkers and action takers who push the new idea through the organization
- A deep understanding of the traditional orthodoxies that need to be overcome

The Tyranny of Experience

Hamel's take on management innovation is typical of his take on any number of devices by which a company sets its course and might be accurately (if too succinctly) summed up as: get outside your comfort zone. "Strategy making should be subversive," he has said. "Great strategies come from challenging the status quo and doing something different."

The impetus to make that happen, he believes, should come from the highest offices: "The bottleneck is at the top of the bottle. The most powerful defenders of strategic orthodoxy are senior management, and strategy making needs to be freed from the tyranny of their experience." To those who grasp their company's strategic processes far too tightly, he advises, "Strategy making is about letting go."

What's the penalty for not letting go? According to Hamel, it's falling prey to the twin killers of success in the twenty-first century: retrenchment and incrementalism. "Most companies don't have any strategy which goes beyond retrenchment," he has asserted. "Retrenchment doesn't buy you growth, it doesn't buy you a future. At best it buys you time."

Incrementalism, in Hamel's opinion, perhaps had its place during the last century. At the beginning of the 1980s, companies aimed for greater size and success through downsizing, flattening, reengineering, and other fad instruments such as total quality.

"Today, the goal of becoming incrementally better is ingrained in our thinking, in our language, in our reward mechanisms, and in everything we do," he asserts, adding that such techniques must be consigned to the dustbin of history. "We have to create new metrics. Most of the metrics that companies use—ROI, EVA, and so on—push us into thinking simply about incremental improvements. We still have a very deep belief in management processes that are the antithesis of innovation."

Such new metrics might best be related somehow to the presence of two interrelated elements: newcomers and passion. Companies need to trust the "new voices" that emerge coincident with "top management relinquishing its hold on strategy and introducing newcomers. Young people and people from different groups bring richness and diversity to strategy formulation." This is, he says, "the only way for incumbents to renew their lease on success. . . . The same people talking the same issues over and over again leads to sterility; new opportunities arise from juxtaposing formerly isolated people."

And when that happens, passion makes its critical contribution to strategy of a uniquely effective sort: "Strategy that is passionately believed in, that is competitively different, and that is articulated in a fine enough grain to act on."

Profound Advantage

In Hamel's corporate world of the twenty-first century, strategy must be directed, above all, toward innovation, and innovation can neither be relegated to departments such as R&D nor be limited to periodic corporate innovation blitzes. Instead, it must be a constant concern in every corner of the company: "My argument is that the more difficult the economic times, the more one is tempted to retrench, the more radical innovation becomes the only way forward. In a discontinuous world, only radical innovation will create new wealth."

Radical innovation isn't your father's innovation, the kind found when "CEOs . . . say that they need to innovate and put innovation as one of their top two or three priorities." The trouble is, Hamel argues, that the buck stops there: "Go down a few levels in the organization and talk to midlevel employees . . . it's obvious that most companies have not institutionalized innovation in a meaningful way. . . . It is not seen as the responsibility of every single employee every single day."

Yet the rewards of making it so are decisive for long-term corporate success: "Companies that commit themselves to innovation—like Whirlpool, Cemex, Shell, and a few others—are going to have a profound advantage. . . . Over the last 40 years, Western car makers haven't recaptured even a single point of market share from their Japanese competitors."

To avoid a similar fate, Hamel says, "requires a fundamental rethinking of your most basic business principles. . . . Innovation has to be central to the purpose of organizations. We have to systematically train people in new ways of thinking. . . . We have to reengineer management processes to minimize the time between an idea and wealth creation. It's not the supply chain that needs shortening and automating, it's the innovation chain that needs shortening and automating. True innovators are never bound by what is; instead, they dream of what could be."

In those dreams, Hamel believes, lies what he calls economic progress.

There's social innovation, institutional innovation, technology innovation, and finally management innovation. It was management innovation that delivered actual economic progress. Until we learned how to bring people together, to do things at scale in highly productive ways, all that other innovation was great, but it didn't fundamentally result in anything that actually changed our standard of living. . . . The evidence would suggest that management innovation—fundamental breakthroughs in how we motivate organize, plan, allocate, evaluate those things—tends to produce longer-lasting advantages.

Totally Rad

Hamel's talk about business innovation in the twenty-first century is punctuated with recurring use of the word *radical*, as in: "Can you envision radical and far-reaching changes in how managers do what they do?"

While corporate chieftains of the Fortune 500 ilk may find the word disquieting, Hamel seems to find it profitably provocative, given that Strategos, the Silicon Valley consulting firm he founded, claims to aid client efforts aimed at achieving "radical innovation."

Hamel warns that radical change and radical innovation are no longer optional for companies. "Could the practice of management change as radically over the first two or three decades of this century as it did during the adolescence of the twentieth century? I believe so. More than that, I believe we must make it so. The challenges facing twenty-first-century business leaders are at least as intimidating, exciting, and unprecedented as those that confronted the world's industrial pioneers a hundred years ago."

One may expect that most corporate leaders, contrary to sentiments expressed by the Beatles, are not among those who would want a revolution that would change the world. Hamel might argue that the world has changed with or without companies' senior management: "Only those companies that are capable of creating industry revolutions will prosper in the new economy."

Hamel sympathizes with the executives' plight: "We've learned how to use our positional prerogatives, our access to power and our polished professionalism, to get ahead," he wrote in *The End of Management.* "Talk about revolution—particularly management revolution—makes us jittery. Who, one wonders, will come out on top if the rules and roles of management are turned upside down? Yet despite our reservations, . . . real progress demands a revolution."

It's no surprise, then, that an earlier Hamel book was *Leading the Revolution,* in which he advised companies to adopt Hamelian prescriptions: Set unreasonable goals. Define the business broadly. Create a cause. Listen to your newcomers. Divide big companies into cells. And so forth.

Hamel seems to think that not many companies will ultimately heed his advice, as he says, "Truly revolutionary, global-scale business models don't come along every day or even every decade." That should keep him in heavy demand for as many more years as he cares to toil.

Hamel on Innovation

Talking with Hamel, we asked:

*What's wrong with management now that we need to
remake it?*
I think we have to start by asking, why did we invent
management in the first place? And we don't often
think about management as a technology, but I argue
that it is a technology: it's the technology of human
accomplishment; it's what we use to do things at
scale as human beings. And management in some
sense goes back as far as recorded history, but really,
modern management got created about 100 or 120
years ago to solve one primary problem, which is how
do you take semiskilled or illiterate people and get
them to do the same things over and over again with
ever-improving efficiency? That was an important
problem to solve. The fact that today you can have
a couple of cars in the garage and a digital device in
every pocket, that you're not spending 80 percent
of your time cultivating your own food, all of this is
thanks to that group of management pioneers who
figured out how to do things at scale in highly productive ways.

Unfortunately, efficiency and simply doing
things on a large scale are no longer the most important problems for most organizations today. They're
worrying about, How do we become more adapt-
able? How do we become more innovative? How do

we truly engage the minds and creative energies of the people who work within our organizations? And these are problems that largely lie outside the scope of our old Management 1.0 model.

You put your reputation where your mouth is and started this Management Innovation Lab, the MLab.
What we really started to ask ourselves was, what is management's equivalent of the human genome project, or putting someone on the moon, or finding a cure for AIDS? Why can't we dramatically change this technology that we so often just take for granted? We perpetuate the practices and principles that have been with us for the last 100 years. So, it's really a project aimed at accelerating the evolution of this technology. And the primary way we're hoping to do that is by creating an open innovation platform where people from around the world can contribute their breakthrough ideas on how we get better at allocating resources, creating our plans, setting direction, measuring performance, compensating, and motivating human beings. But what we're really trying to do is create an opportunity for anybody around the world to have the chance to hack management, if you will.

And we're talking specifically about management innovation, which is different from innovation per se. Can you explain exactly what the difference is?
Yes. I think we can think almost of a hierarchy of innovation, if you will. At the bottom is operational

innovation—the things that organizations do every day to get incrementally more efficient and more productive; a lot of stuff goes on around IT, customer support, and so on. A level up from that, you have product innovation of the sort that delivers the latest flat-screen television or some new financial instrument. Above that, you have business model innovation, which created Facebook, IKEA, Southwest Airlines—pick your example.

But really at the top you have management innovation—fundamental breakthroughs in the way we organize human beings in productive ways. And if you go back over the last 100 or so years of industrial history, what you'll find is that the most significant and enduring shifts in competitive advantage came not from innovation in products, technology, or business models, but from innovation in management itself.

So, management innovation is anything that changes the way the work of management gets done (how we allocate, plan, direct, and so on) or changes who does that work. And in an organization of any size, the only way you change the work of management is by changing the processes, the routines that govern the way that work gets done: how you submit a budget requisition, how you evaluate an employee, and so on. So, management innovation is really focused on those core management processes that drive the organization forward.

Can you give some examples?

Let me pick three or four examples that would be clear standouts. Back at the very beginning of the twentieth century, General Electric worked with Thomas Edison to invent the world's first R&D labs. People had been doing science for a long time, but GE brought management discipline to science. So Edison could say, we can now create a minor breakthrough every six weeks and a major breakthrough every six months. No one before had ever put science on a schedule, and within a couple of decades, GE had more industrial patents than any company in the world.

You go forward a decade or so, a couple of decades, and General Motors was this big, sprawling empire, with no economies of scale or scope. The chairman at the time turned to a young staffer, Alfred Sloan, and said, "How do we get some order to this chaos?" And he invented the notion of the divisionalized organization—centralized finance policy, but decentralized operations. That has become the template for every multibusiness company since. Every large organization has some General Motors DNA in it. Sadly, that was the last time GM was a bona fide management innovator.

Coming a bit more recently, 37 years ago, one of Toyota's great breakthroughs was the notion of employee-focused problem solving. So, how do you take first-line employees, teach them statistical process control and Pareto analysis, and hold them responsible for improving quality, efficiency, and so on over time? This is a radical break with the past.

More recently, we see things like open innovation. I think that even a decade ago, if we'd surveyed a thousand CEOs across the world and said, "Can you foresee a time when a ragtag collection of volunteers around the world with little in the way of hierarchy or formal management processes will be able to create things as complex as a computer operating system with millions of lines of code?," many of them would have had a hard time imagining that this could be true. So those are a few examples of the signal changes in how we think about management. And when you go back and look at how a lot of those changes happened, you find that it often involved a fairly tight collaboration between a very progressive manager and often somebody out of the academic world, like Frederick Taylor or W. Edwards Deming, working together to really experiment and try things.

And sadly, I think, over the last couple of decades, we've lost that experimental sense of let's just go try new things in the way we manage, lead, organize, plan, and allocate. And part of what I'm hoping to do, both inside organizations and very much in the community of management faculty, is to rekindle that spirit of adventure and experimentation in how we do the work of management.

Is that because people are under too much pressure now? Is it because we've got this short-termism, with

CEOs constantly having to report to Wall Street and say, "Profits are up again"? Does that not give us any space to experiment?

I think that certainly pressures organizations, and sometimes it makes it difficult to try things that don't have an immediate payoff. But I would have said that the much bigger thing holding us back is our own embedded management models. The fact of the matter is, if you think of management as a technology, if you plotted its evolution over the last 100 years or so, you'd find that it follows this very classic S-curve where there's a lot of innovation in the beginning and then it flattens out.

Certainly over my lifetime, the way we manage our organizations has changed hardly at all. If we could somehow resurrect a 1960s-era CEO and put him back in the executive suite, there are certain things that would surprise him—the 24/7 pace of business, the amount of information he had at his fingertips—but much of the way we manage would be very familiar to him. The hierarchy still looks pretty much the way it always did, people with big titles and big positions still make the big decisions, power pretty much flows from the top down, credentials determine share of voice, budgeting works the way it always has, and so on. And indeed, when you go from organization to organization even today, you find that the technology of management varies only slightly from firm to firm.

That's why a CEO can go from one industry to another—somebody can go from running Nokia to being the chairman of Shell—and when she walks into the executive suite, the levers and dials are pretty much in the same place. Which, by the way, is another way of saying that most organizations don't have a management advantage; despite all the work and all the energy they put into all those processes, very little of that creates anything that's truly distinctive in terms of organizational capability.

But why has management stopped evolving? There are a couple of possible hypotheses. One is that we've solved all the really tough problems: we know how to run these great global organizations with people all over the world and we can coordinate massive projects, so there's nothing really new to be done anymore. I think the second and more likely hypothesis is that we're all just being held hostage by the same set of hand-me-down beliefs that we inherited from ex-CEOs, management gurus, and pioneers, most of whom are long dead, long retired, or long in the tooth. But we've just assumed that this is the only way to do it until somebody comes along and says maybe there's a different way here.

Rescuing Management

As Hamel's observations suggest, in recent times, management has been downplayed to such an extent that it often appears peripheral and deeply rooted in tedious bureaucracy. This does management a grave disservice. It is important.

"For many people today, the word *management* conjures up images of hierarchy, control and formal procedures, for reasons that have nothing to do with the underlying meaning of the term. 'Management' and 'large industrial firm' became intertwined in the 1920s, and they are still tightly linked today," laments Julian Birkinshaw.

> Such a narrow model of management blinds us to the range of alternative management models that exist. Sports teams, social communities, aid organizations (even families) operate with very different principles from large industrial companies, and these alternative principles are potentially very useful today.
>
> This narrow definition also leads us to assume, incorrectly, that large industrial companies are inherently superior to other forms of organization. Yes, there are certain industrial processes that are best suited to economies of scale and scope, but we would be misunderstanding history if we assumed that mass production was the only feasible model of industrial organization. We need to recognize that management models other than the hierarchical, bureaucratic organization have their own important merits.

Management is alive and well, but it is no longer the management created and modeled by Henry Ford, Alfred P. Sloan, and the like. It is more fluid, flexible, and powerful than ever before—more innovative.

Leading
Innovation

In the past, a CEO's view of innovation was often limited to the budget allocated to the company's R&D division. R&D was a distant organizational specter, somehow beyond the conventional reach or understanding of the company's leaders.

Now, with innovation having become an issue for the CEO, providing leadership to those who are charged with innovating is part and parcel of senior management's responsibility. The trouble is that those who work in innovation often defy traditional leadership. They are smart, are experts in their fields, and often consider their peers to be the equally smart people doing similar things in other organizations rather than executives in their own organization.

The challenge in providing leadership to these groups is powerfully mapped out by Rob Goffee and Gareth Jones in *Clever*. "How do you corral a group of extremely smart and highly creative individuals into an organization, and then inspire them not only to achieve their fullest potential as individuals, but to do so in a way that creates wealth and value for all your stakeholders?" they ask.

If there's one defining characteristic of these people, it is that they claim they do not want to be led. Clearly, this poses an enormous challenge for corporate leaders. Smart executives may not have the answers to all the questions, but the best of them understand the problem of not effectively managing their intellectual know-how and those who generate it.

Jonothan Neelands is professor of creative education at Warwick Business School. He argues that organizations need to create open spaces to nurture innovation and creativity. This, he says, is based on three concepts:

The first concept is *flow*. Originally proposed by the Hungarian psychologist Mihaly Csíkszentmihályi, flow is the mental state of operation in which a person performing an activity is fully immersed in a feeling of energized focus, full involvement, and enjoyment in the process of the activity. Think of losing yourself in playing music or writing, or in playing a sport. According to Csíkszentmihályi, flow is completely focused motivation, so that the self is immersed in the activity.

Open spaces are usually spaces shared with other actors or colleagues, so there is also openness in terms of how we dwell together in creative spaces. Flow is the desired state that we aspire to.

This raises important questions for businesses. In particular, what forms of cooperation foster social creativity? The mood of learning, working, creating in open spaces is subjunctive—full of possibilities, imaginings, what-ifs, maybes, and possible beginnings.

At best, it is a cooperative space without coercion or external legislation. We capitalize on our strengths and differences. It is a differentiated mode of exchange. It is also a public rather than an intimate space; we come wearing the neutral masks of the citizen, the disinterested professional, or the craftsperson. It is important that we do so, and that our cooperation is indirect and impersonal.

In essence, being in flow is accepting that nothing is predetermined or set in stone. We—and our business processes—are in a fluid rather than a solid state.

Closely related to flow, the second concept implicit in open space learning is that of *playfulness*.

The key to social transformations on the scale required to meet the demands of the twenty-first century is understanding how to utilize, in our adult world, the playful strategies of children, both with objects and the pursuit of socially playful goals and in their innate uses of the imagination.

There are connections between children's uses of play, the play of a company of actors in producing a play, and the possibility that play as an attitude to process rather than as an event may offer a model to other groups that are intent on creative invention.

So play is also a preparation for the necessity of repetition and modulation in creative training and work. Because there is no penalty for not achieving a predetermined goal in play, children learn to succeed through constant repetition and modulation. They practice for hours with the same Lego or clay, for instance, in the same way that an artist must practice for hours to create original music.

Along with flow and playfulness, the third principle of open space learning is *togetherness*, or working as part of an ensemble. This is where personal or individual creativity crosses the line into business creativity. In the workplace, we need to work as part of the larger organization. Even though there are opportunities for individual creative brilliance, the creative ego needs to be harnessed to—or engaged by—the organizational goals.

One of the first and most important aspects of this sort of togetherness is the setting aside of hierarchical position. So, in open space learning, there are flexible and less hierarchical uses of space, and knowledge is considered provisional, problematic, and unfinished. There is often an "uncrowning" of the power of the teacher, leader, or director and an expectation that learning, or rehearsal, will be negotiated and co-constructed. Open space learning requires trust and mutuality among participants; the circle is its essential shape. Crucially, the space is open to others; it is a shared public space that is set up in order to negotiate meanings socially and artistically.

Organizing for Innovation

Creating organizations along these lines is difficult for companies that have been reared on traditional twentieth-century thinking. In the search for alternative models, one of the most popular sources of inspiration is the world of design. Roger Martin has championed design thinking, and the approach of the world-famous design firm IDEO has been justly celebrated.

IDEO emerged from a business begun by Bill Moggridge in London in the 1960s. As British industry hit the rocks in the late 1970s, Moggridge looked elsewhere for work. He found himself in Silicon Valley, where things were just beginning to get interesting. Moggridge hooked up with another designer, the American David Kelley. Before long, Moggridge and Kelley's companies were supplemented by a spin-off company run by another British designer, Mike Nuttall. The companies then combined as IDEO.

IDEO has quietly thrived. Along the way, it has survived being labeled one of the world's coolest companies to work for and has survived eulogies from the American guru Tom Peters. "It's finally happened. I've seen a company where I can imagine working," pronounced Peters upon visiting IDEO's Palo Alto office for the first time.

The company is different not because of its designs—innovative though they are—but because of its culture. While copying IDEO's designs would be largely pointless and potentially illegal, seeking to emulate its culture may make a great deal of sense—although, of course, it is the most demanding thing to copy.

IDEO practices grown-up management. Its innovation is the way it works and the way it is. The first notable thing about the company is that it has not expanded at breakneck speed. Indeed, by most measures, it has hardly expanded at all. Despite being internationally lauded and profitable, IDEO has relatively few employees.

The second key to grown-up management is that IDEO is based around projects. In keeping with its unwillingness to embrace growth for its own sake, multiskilled project teams change from project to project. Projects are its culture.

The company's folklore (captured in Tom Kelley's book *The Art of Innovation*) is brimming with stories of supermarket trolleys being redesigned in a week and how the company developed the first Apple computer mouse. Amid stories of developing the first single-use instant camera, creating all-terrain eyewear, and reinventing the light switch, there is no mention of costs and profits. The unspoken understanding is that brilliant, problem-solving design makes money for the company and its clients. It is user-based design. At the heart of the business is using design thinking to help clients be more valuable.

Another core element of the IDEO culture is the concept of the studio. The IDEO-style studio is not a production line with an all-knowing, all-seeing font of creativity standing at one end. The star designer does not breeze in and out while a tribe of assistants labors over his latest creation. Most design companies are based on a single individual and fail when that individual moves on. Others are based on confrontation. IDEO works through open critiques of people's work. Its belief is that part of being a studio is defending what you believe to be true.

The makeup of IDEO's staff has subtly evolved, particularly over recent years. The power of IDEO was to take what otherwise might have been quite a "siloed" situation—designers don't talk to engineers, and neither group will talk to human factors people—and create a culture in which team members respect one another.

In many ways, the design studio, as practiced at IDEO, is an organizational model that is in tune with our times. For one thing, it is small and creative. It is also low on hierarchy and big on communication, and it requires a minimal amount of ego. IDEO's designers may take the starring role in a particular project and then find themselves back in the chorus on the next project.

Sustaining this culture requires dedication rather than innovative wackiness. It starts in the recruitment process. Compared to those of many other organizations, IDEO's recruitment process is long and drawn out. There are three or four interviews. Applicants then show their work and discuss it with a group of IDEO people. Then they get to meet everyone and look at the projects that are underway to see how they interact. This is time-consuming, but essential, says IDEO. It wants to know how well people will fit. The teams have a say.

The rigor that IDEO brings to recruitment is increasingly matched by the attention it pays to evaluating performance. It has annual formal reviews based on a matrix of five elements: content, culture (team working and team leadership), client, commerce, and mentoring and leadership.

The Innovation Route

The ideal environment for creativity and innovation, suggested by IDEO and others, is far removed from corporate reality. Clearly, this has enormous repercussions for how companies should be organized and led if they want to be innovative.

So, how do you provide the best leadership for innovation?

Providing intellectual leadership on this tortured subject is Linda Hill, the Wallace Brett Donham Professor of Business Administration at Harvard Business School. She is the coauthor, with Kent Lineback, of *Being the Boss* and author of *Becoming a Manager*. More recently, her research (along with Greg Brandeau, Kent Lineback, and Emily Stecker Truelove) has looked at exceptional leaders of innovation in a wide range of industries—from IT to law to design—throughout the world.

Hill describes herself as an ethnographer. She is now in her thirtieth year at Harvard Business School and has twice been shortlisted for Thinkers50 awards.

What is the focus of your research?

I study three things: how people learn to lead, how people lead innovation, and implementing global strategies. I've always worked on all three of those to some extent, but the one that means the most to me is leading innovation.

Because of that, one of our former deans asked me to do a couple of things. Given that our mission is to educate leaders to make a difference in the world, he asked me to help create our first required course on leadership. I led the team. Second, he asked me to help develop our e-learning strategy. This was at the end of the 1990s, so he was really quite a visionary in understanding that education was going to go down that route, that we needed to be able to use the Internet to deliver educational experiences, both here on campus and also, more important, to people around the world. That was great for me.

Your work is notably international.
I am usually out of the country about twice a month, certainly when I'm not teaching. My father was in the military, and so I went to high school in Bangkok and grew up thinking about the world. I went to India for the first time when I was 14, and I've always had this sense of wanting to be out and about and feeling that there are lots of interesting people in the world.

I'm a business professor because I fundamentally am interested in economic development. My PhD is in behavioral sciences, which is an interdisciplinary degree, but I'm actually more of a sociologist than a psychologist.

My parents come from modest backgrounds, and I didn't really know about business per se. My relatives were coal miners or worked on the factory floor, so I didn't really know about business.

What I've always been interested in is, how do you create organizations that allow people to fulfill their ambitions? The only organizations I knew were educational ones. I studied learning theory in college and then went to the University of Chicago, where I met Jacob Getzels, who is considered to be the father of research on creativity.

Actually, the first research project I ever did was a study on creativity and brainstorming as a freshman at Bryn Mawr College.

So, all my life I've been interested in creativity. Mr. Getzels [coauthor of *Creativity and Intelligence* in 1962], as we called him, was one of the founders of creativity research. He was very interested in how you design educational institutions that allow people to be creative. I worked on his projects, and one of them involved studying artists at the Art Institute of Chicago to see who was the most creative and why, and how the organizational setting affected their creativity.

At that time, creativity wasn't really taken seriously or looked at.

Mr. Getzels used to tell me, "Any theory you have, Linda, if it's a good theory, it will help people solve a practical problem." So he helped me understand that there was really no difference between rigor and relevance. You couldn't be relevant without being rigorous, and how could you be rigorous about something that wasn't relevant, that wouldn't solve a problem?

I was interested in wicked social problems, and how people could, by being creative, help solve those problems. So I've always gone between business and other sectors because I'm really interested in economic development and how you help improve people's lives and livelihoods. Harvard Business School has been a fabulous platform for me, letting me be able to move around and do the things I wanted to do, from being on the board of the Rockefeller Foundation and learning about how you create organizations to come up with an AIDS vaccine, to trying to help a businessperson figure out something.

And all of this leads to your current work.
Yes. Greg Brandeau, the former chief technology officer of Pixar, Kent Lineback, Emily Stecker Truelove, and I have spent six years traveling the world, studying 16 leaders who created teams at organizations that were able to routinely innovate.

In a way, this project started when I was asked to write a piece on what I thought leadership would look like in the twenty-first century. I had been the faculty chair of a required course on leadership for nine years or so, and I had become concerned that we might not be developing the kind of leaders we need.

I was spending a fair amount of time in South Africa and had the privilege of meeting some people who had been in prison with Nelson Mandela, and then I met Mandela himself. I wrote about Nelson Mandela and his notions of leadership.

Then I met someone who was running Google's infrastructure group. There was an interesting connection between what it means to lead a revolution and what it means to lead a major innovation. These people who were running these very innovative groups thought about leadership in the same way.

Mandela says that a leader is like a shepherd. He stays behind the flock, letting the most nimble go on ahead whereupon others follow, not realizing that all along they are being directed from behind. And people leading innovative groups say much the same thing: it's not about me saying, "This is where we need to go, and you follow me," and me inspiring you to follow me, because fundamentally, I don't know the answer. I don't know where we're going. So that's not what leadership is about. It's about creating these teams or groups where people are willing and able to do innovative problem solving together, and so we're trying to provide an integrated model for thinking about that.

What really struck me is that no one really writes about what leaders do and how they think about leadership when innovation is their primary concern.

Leadership really began to be seriously studied at business schools only at the beginning of the 1990s.
Yes. People ended up thinking that leadership is about being visionary. But when you're talking about innovation, that whole charismatic visionary thing is a problem. Most innovations are the result of collaborative efforts, discovery-driven learning, and more integrated decision making. The tasks, roles, and responsibilities of leaders and followers are very different when you really think about innovation as your goal, about discovering something that doesn't exist at the moment, about solving problems.

One of the things you always hear about leadership is that despite all the executive programs, all the training, and all the books, there's a shortage of leaders. And similarly with innovation; despite all the books on and study of innovation, it remains largely a mystery to most organizations.

Yes. I think that is because people don't really understand the connection between leadership, what leaders think they're supposed to be doing, and what it actually takes to build an organization that can be innovative. They're disconnected disciplines. I don't think we have much insight into what an individual leader should be doing or thinking about, or how people should think about what the role of that leader should be if she wants to be innovative.

Everybody has a slice of genius in his organization. How do you combine those slices of genius in integrated ways to come up with solutions to problems? Some people would say, you don't want that many geniuses, because then there's the too-many-cooks-in-the-kitchen problem. Well, there are organizations that have figured out how you can have lots of cooks in the kitchen and still have them cook an absolutely fabulous meal.

Pixar has been a very successful studio, financially, artistically, and technologically, and that really goes back to how the people there think about leadership. No place is perfect, but Pixar has a certain way of thinking about what it's up to and what leadership is about that has allowed it to create a community culture with the capabilities that are essential for innovative problem solving.

What surprised you along the way with the research?
Well, there were two things. The first big one was that the fields of leadership and innovation were so separate, so very siloed.

The other was that when we first went through the data, we picked up themes about the norms in the organizations, about how you're supposed to interact with people or how you're supposed to treat people. What we didn't pick up on until we began to look a little bit more at the capabilities of these organizations was that there were also norms about how you're supposed to think about a problem. So that was a surprise. As we tried to explain what we were seeing in certain settings, we said, "This isn't about how you interact with people; this is really about how you frame and solve problems." Because these organizations have some norms about how you're supposed to think about problems, and that's one of the things that allows them to get through the too-many-cooks-in-the-kitchen problem.

In many ways, it seems that we have preferred a simple explanation of how leading innovation works rather than the complex reality.
I think that people like simple, relatively speaking. Things need to be simpler as opposed to more complex, and this led to the worshipping of a myth about

how innovation happens. Albert Einstein did not work alone and have an aha experience. Innovation is collaborative. Howard Gardner talks about the social process and the environment that affects creativity.

I think leading change is different from leading innovation. So there's not one right way to lead in all circumstances, and a lot of the work on leadership versus management came from organizations that were failing suddenly and had to be revived and turned around. Change is not exactly the same as innovation. They're somewhat different issues.

How does this work relate to your book Being the Boss?

In *Being the Boss*, the second imperative was managing your network. Many people, when they think about leadership, think only about managing people over whom they have formal authority. But in today's organization, you also need to think about managing people that you don't have formal authority over.

It came from me talking to a lot of my former students and executives I worked with and seeing their common missteps. Why weren't they realizing their potential, and why weren't they powerful? They weren't thinking about leadership in a way that helped them really address what they needed to—that it's about yourself, your network, and your team.

CHAPTER 8

Where Innovation Meets Strategy

As we have seen, innovation and strategy once existed in isolation. Innovation was the preserve of a distant R&D department, whereas strategy was the responsibility of senior executives at headquarters.

No more. Now the two are regarded as bedfellows, sometimes awkwardly so, but often powerfully.

Bridging the gap between strategy and innovation are the ideas of Professor W. Chan Kim and his INSEAD colleague, Professor Renée Mauborgne. They have probably done more to change our perception of how strategy and innovation fit together than any other thinkers in recent decades. To date, their 2005 book *Blue Ocean Strategy* has sold more than two million copies and has been translated into 43 languages, making it, by some measures at least, the most successful business book of all time.

"We started off by looking at the companies that succeeded in circumventing the competition," explains Professor Kim. "Then we moved on to how to create new market space—companies need a way to think and act out of the box if they are to circumvent the competition. Our notion of 'fair process' looks at management decision making and what is required to build and execute creative thinking. Most recently we have looked at how to identify a winning business idea and determine which one to bet on. Qualifying an innovative idea for commercial success is a critical strategy component of value innovation."

How do you define value innovation?

Mauborgne: Value innovation is creating an unprecedented set of utilities at a lower cost. It is not about making trade-offs, but about simultaneously pursuing both exceptional value and lower costs. . . . The power of value innovation is in engaging people to build collective wisdom in a constructive manner. Value innovation means that the range of disagreement becomes smaller until creativity explodes. Value innovation is fundamentally concerned with redefining the established boundaries of a market. If you offer buyers hugely improved value or create an unprecedented set of utilities in order to give birth to new markets, then the competition becomes unimportant. Instead of playing on the same field, you have created a new one.

Value innovation enables companies to shift the productivity frontier to a new terrain. Value improvements get you only so far. Value innovation is concerned with challenging accepted assumptions about particular markets, changing the way managers frame the strategic possibilities.

Is the driving force behind value innovation the willingness of companies to create new markets?
Mauborgne: Fundamentally. Innovation occurs across industries, across countries, across companies. These are universal forces. It is, therefore, irrelevant to categorize organizations by their sector or geographical location. Yet, if you look at strategy literature, industry boundaries are usually regarded as central—think of SWOT analysis or Michael Porter's Five Forces Framework.[1]

Making the Right Moves

Another thinker who is standing at the intersection of strategy and innovation is Costas Markides. Markides is a professor of strategic and international management and holds the Robert P. Bauman Chair in Strategic Leadership at the London Business School.

"The one thing I have learned from two decades of study," he says, "is that innovation and continued success depend on the leader of the organization being willing to take drastic action, even when the organization is doing very well."

Won't that draw howls of protest from shareholders, analysts, and other key constituencies? Yes, Markides admits,

"And yet, that's exactly the right time for organizations to rejuvenate themselves. The problem with companies is that, when they are on the upswing, they never introduce change. When do they introduce change? When they are down, and then it's often too late."

Markides, the author of *All the Right Moves: A Guide to Crafting Breakthrough Strategy* (2000); *Fast Second: How Smart Companies Bypass Radical Innovation to Enter and Dominate New Markets* (with Paul Geroski, 2005); and *Game-Changing Strategies: How to Create New Market Space in Established Industries by Breaking the Rules* (2008), explores the challenge of how established firms can innovate their business model, as well as how to respond to the threat from the introduction of a new business model.

Build a Wall

Markides asserts that the skills, mindsets, and attitudes required for breakthrough innovation not only are different from those required for continuing success in existing markets, but also conflict with them. Firms that are good at the former are unlikely to be good at the latter.

What's more, big, established companies do not have the skills and mindsets needed for creating radically new markets, nor can they easily develop those skills and mindsets, because they conflict with the skills and mindsets that the companies have and need in their existing businesses. However, these corporations do have the skills and mindsets that are needed for taking new market niches developed by others and scaling them up into mass markets.

How can we reconcile these differences? Markides's recommendation is to keep the established and the entrepreneurial apart. Draw a line. Build a wall. The exact character of the division is whichever of numerous alternatives might work for the company.

Markides employs much the same reasoning in warning established companies away from the so-called first-mover advantage—so much so, in fact, that he, along with Paul Geroski, rejected the notion of there being an advantage to being a first mover. He contends that the skill sets of most established companies are far better suited to scaling up newly created markets that were pioneered by others.

"Look at Microsoft," Markides says. "What did it create? The answer is basically nothing. What Microsoft did was take the creations of others and scale them up into mass markets." This is not a bad thing, according to Markides. Non–first movers such as Microsoft are what Markides calls *fast seconds*. The firms that create new markets are rarely the ones that scale them into mass markets. That is the realm of fast seconds.

The fast second, according to Markides, can adeptly slip into and own a new market. "The skills, mindsets, and competencies needed for discovery and invention not only are different from those needed for commercialization," he contends, "but also conflict with the needed characteristics. This means that firms that are good at invention are unlikely to be good at commercialization and vice versa."

Under this construct, Markides favors a more expansive view of what constitutes innovation. "I believe innovation is two things—the creation of something, and also, and more important, the commercialization, the scaling up, of that something."

With this perspective on innovation, the continuous innovation imperative for established firms is not what it is usually presumed to be: creating radical new business models. In fact, it is not in the realm of creativity at all, but rather in that of taking the creations of others and scaling them up to mass market status.

That task, which Markides calls commercialization, is the specialty of fast seconds. Unfortunately, they often waste resources on efforts to match the creative achievements of innovating start-ups. Such attempts, Markides believes, are futile. They reveal not creativity but corporate arrogance—and all for nothing.

Fast seconds should instead understand that their core competency is in consolidation and be content to capitalize on that. In fact, Markides notes, "That's where the money is." That doesn't mean that established companies can't guarantee their access to radical innovations. They can "create, sustain, and nurture a network of feeder firms." The parent consolidator, Markides asserts, "can serve as a venture capitalist to these feeder firms." When it's time to consolidate, the parent can build a new mass market business on the platform that the feeder firms provide.

Conflicting Business Models

Big, established companies are also frequently attacked by bold start-ups that succeed in grabbing market share by employing entirely new business models. Markides acknowledges that new business models can create entirely new markets, "so they are good innovations to have."

Problems arise, however, because "established companies are generally poor at discovering new business models." What's more, "they also have a terrible time responding to the ones that newcomers use to attack established markets."

Markides notes that this is to be expected. "New business models conflict with the established business models of established firms"—for example, there are cannibalization conflicts, distribution conflicts, cultural conflicts, incentive conflicts, and so forth. "This implies that no matter how much good advice you give established firms on discovering new business models," Markides explains, "they are highly unlikely to do so. Why discover something that will destroy my existing business or alienate my existing distributors?"

So, if the established firm won't succeed by responding to a disruptive competitor's new business model with its own new business model, what response might succeed? Markides suggests two possible responses: "disrupt the disruptor or play two games at the same time."

As to the first of these, "The established companies that respond successfully look at the disrupter and determine what they can do to disrupt it." That's what Nintendo accomplished with its successful Wii. Nintendo "was a traditional established competitor" in electronic games when "Sony and Microsoft attacked Nintendo's lead with PlayStation and the Xbox."

If Nintendo had followed the usual established firm's response, it would have left the market entirely or played Sony's and Microsoft's game (literally) with PlayStation and Xbox imitations. Instead, "Nintendo came up with the Wii, a nontraditional product that emphasizes entirely different dimensions of electronic games." The result was a market niche that was wholly owned by Nintendo, and two disruptors that were quite conclusively disrupted.

As for playing two games at once, the perils that threaten the success of this strategy are many. "In fact," Markides writes, "there are many examples of companies that have pursued this

strategy and failed (such as British Airways with its Go Fly subsidiary and KLM with its Buzz subsidiary), while other companies, such as Nintendo and Mercedes, have succeeded in playing
two games without creating separate units. . . . Only a handful
of companies that created separate units were successful in playing two games." That handful, Markides says, explored five key
questions that could improve the odds of success in competing
with dual business models in the same industry:

- Should I enter the market space created by the new
  business model?
- If I do enter the new market space, can I do it with my
  existing business model, or will I need a new one?
- If I need a new business model to exploit the new market, should I simply adopt the invading business model
  that's disrupting my market?
- If I develop a new business model, how separate should
  it be organizationally from the existing business model?
- Once I create a separate unit, what are the unique challenges of pursuing two business models at once?

Out of the Jungle

In conversation, Costas Markides is excitably persuasive. We
talked first about the sometimes fraught relationship between
strategy and innovation.

> *What is the relationship between strategy and
> innovation? And how important are both in order
> to compete in today's marketplace?*

If the economic environment is good and everybody
is growing, you can grow without even having a strat-

egy. But if you are in a jungle, if you are in a crisis, that's exactly when you need a strategy. But looking beyond strategy, innovation is the first step a company should take.

Why innovation?

I've always believed that innovation is the answer to every organizational problem, because innovation is about growth. If you think about it, if the people operating a business are not growing, innovation will not happen. I've been studying innovation for 20 years, and most people would agree that it's a very crowded field.

Are there ways in which your approach to innovation is different?

There are two areas where I think I bring a differentiating element to the core study of innovation. The first is that when you look at the work of other academics and consultants, they talk about innovation in general. I believe that there are different kinds of innovation, and that the mechanism you need if you are to achieve one kind of innovation is different from the mechanism you need if you are to pursue another kind of innovation.

Can you clarify that point?

For example, my last book was on business model innovation—how companies develop new business models—and I wrote about what companies need to do to achieve that. My previous book was about radical product innovation and how to come up with new radical products. My prescription for how to achieve radical product innovation is totally different from that for how to achieve business model innovation. So, I don't think it's right to talk about innovation in general and tell managers that any one approach is what they need to use in order to become more innovative. Those who study innovation and those who try to help companies to innovate need to be more specific about what kind of innovation is most needed and then give companies the appropriate advice. That's one of the things that I do with my innovation work that separates me from others.

And the second way that you are different?

The other thing that I think differentiates my work is my view that innovation is much more than creativity. A lot of published work is about how companies can come up with new ideas about business models, about products—about anything; and brainstorming, visioning, and breakthrough thinking are helpful in generating new ideas. However, even though I think it's important to come up with new ideas and it's an important part of the innovation process, it's not enough. Most of the problems arise after people in business come up with the radical new ideas; what really determines whether a company is innovative or not occurs in the implementation stage.

You're saying that it's not just coming up with a new idea: you have to put it into practice.

Absolutely. For example, let's say you operate an established company, and you devise a new business model. The issue for you is not only how to come up with the new business model, but what to do with the old one. Do you abandon the old one (the way you operate your business today) so that you can move 100 percent into the new one? Or, do you continue with the existing business model while also phasing in the new one; and if you do this, how do you operate with two business models at the same time? That's where I try to focus my work: on the implementation issues of innovation.

How many different kinds of innovation are there?

At the very least, I think companies need to start thinking about product innovation being different from technological innovation, from process innovation, and from business model innovation. For me, those are the four big ones. I'm sure there are more and finer divisions that others could cut innovation into.

Is implementation the point at which most innovations fail?

Absolutely. The problem for companies is not so much coming up with new ideas. When I go into companies and ask the senior managers what they need to do to achieve a certain kind of innovation, amazing as it sounds, they can tell me in five minutes. They don't need to read any books; they don't need to go to visit any other business. Minutes after I ask what needs to be done to innovate, managers can (and do) tell me, "We need to do X, Y, and Z." Then I usually move on from there and ask them, "Well, in this X, Y, Z, have you taken this step or have you initiated that action?" In more cases than not, they have no answer. That's why I say that new ideas are just one part of innovation. New ideas are exciting because they are usually accompanied by new knowledge. But the problem for managers is not knowledge. The problem is action. Innovation is difficult because people usually know what they have to do to achieve it, but they still do not do it.

That behavior seems to work against the best interests of the company and everyone who works there. Why does this happen?
Managers do things that are based on their past experience and habits, repetitive things, but innovation is something that requires the people inside a business to do something completely different. Innovation can require, quite possibly, changing the culture, changing the way managers or others work, and so on. Innovation means change. Managers are very good at doing better and working harder at what they've always done. Innovation is about doing things in a way that is slightly or radically different, and that's where the problem is.

Then how does one begin to innovate?

First of all, at the very minimum, an organization has to put in place an environment that supports and nurtures innovation; and by an environment, I mean a certain culture with certain kinds of incentives along with certain processes that promote innovation. That's the very minimum. But when I tell companies that they have to establish these things, some managers sometimes develop the attitude that the organizational environment must be completely right before innovation can occur.

And it doesn't?

I can give lots of examples of organizations in which the culture and the structures were not optimal, and yet certain individuals took it upon themselves to drive innovation. So, ideally, companies need the right culture and incentives and structures, but over and above that, they need individuals who are willing to go beyond the constraints that any organization places upon them in order to take action—to start working on the X, Y, and Z that I cited earlier. Sadly, there are very few people out there who are willing to stick their necks out and really do things differently.

Do you consider yourself innovative?

I would certainly describe myself as a creative person in that I do come up with a lot of ideas, but, by definition, I'm an academic, and we are not very good at implementing things. So, I wouldn't say I'm an innovator. *Innovator*, for me, means someone who comes up with new ideas and implements them to derive new value. The first half is creative thinking; the second is action; both of them together is innovation.

How do you generate your ideas about strategy and innovation?

I get ideas by working with people (such as senior managers), by writing cases on organizations, and by observing problems that organizations have in day-to-day life. For example, many companies want to get people to cooperate and not allow themselves to become locked in organizational silos, which is a big problem in many businesses. In such cases, I usually ask senior managers how many of them have two, three, or more children. Almost all of them do, so then I ask whether their children cooperate. "Yes," they say. Then I ask whether their children operate in little silos. Their reply: "No, it's amazing how they all cooperate." At this point I try to get them to explore what it is they do as parents to encourage their children to cooperate. I mean, it's common sense, isn't it? At the end of the day, there are things that you do at home to get people to cooperate; these actions are exactly the same things that I think you need to do to get cooperation in an organization.

You think outside the organizational box, don't you?

Yes, and I advise others to do the same. Look beyond companies. Look beyond the business environment.

You will be amazed if you let your thinking venture into nontraditional business environments, such as the family; you'll find that you get lots of ideas for what people need to do in the business environment to achieve some of the things they want to achieve. Consider a business school such as London Business School, where you have a class of 50 to 60 students from 50 or 60 countries with different backgrounds and so on; such diversity should be a fertile ground for idea generation, idea promotion, and things like that. That helps keep my thinking fresh.

Then you certainly value new ideas.

As I mentioned, new ideas are the starting point for innovation. At the end of the day, innovation boils down to an individual's having an open mind and looking for ideas everywhere. Ideas *are* everywhere— in the business world, in the family, in the economic environment; everywhere you look, there are new ideas, new ways of thinking about or doing things. It's just a matter of having an open mind to absorb new ideas and to utilize them for those management applications that can help business prosper. If you can engage new ideas and put them into action in order to serve customers and society in better ways, you'll find that innovation truly is the answer to almost every problem facing your business.

Where Innovation Meets Society

In addition to meeting the pressing demands of business, innovation is also increasingly valued in other walks of life. There is a growing recognition that innovation and progress are inextricably linked. Many (perhaps all) of the challenges confronting us personally, nationally, and globally require innovative solutions. New ways of looking at the world may yield innovative approaches for tackling so-called wicked problems such as global warming and world poverty. New ideas are coalescing around these challenges. Social innovation—the idea that society itself can be improved through innovation—is a concept that is gaining currency.

At the other extreme, too, there is a growing sense that we as individuals can benefit from innovation in our working and nonworking lives. Employee engagement is coming to the fore. Indeed, where people once felt it necessary to preserve two separate lives—professional and personal, with correspondingly compartmentalized identities—these artificial boundaries are merging into what some call whole lives: a more holistic, rounded view of an individual and his or her identity. Human beings, it turns out, want to bring their humanity to work. They want roles that allow them to express themselves and find significance. Organizations that help them do so will reap the dividends of that most human of qualities: ingenuity.

Innovation for Life

Teresa Amabile is the Edsel Bryant Ford Professor of Business Administration in the Entrepreneurial Management Unit at Harvard Business School, and also a director of research at the school. While she is well known for her work on creativity, she has recently focused more broadly on organizational life and its influence on people and their performance.

Amabile is the author and coauthor of a number of books, including *The Progress Principle: Using Small Wins to Ignite Joy, Engagement, and Creativity at Work* (2011). Her previous books include *Creativity in Context: Update to the Social Psychology of Creativity* (1996) and *Growing Up Creative: Nurturing a Lifetime of Creativity* (1989).

In *The Progress Principle*, coauthored with Steven Kramer, Amabile shows how apparently insignificant everyday events in the workplace can affect individuals' working lives and performance. The book draws on the findings from a long-running multistudy research program, including analysis of some 12,000 diary entries from more than 200 employees in seven companies.

What, ask Amabile and Kramer, is the most important factor in employee engagement? Is it incentives, recognition for good work, support for making progress in the work, interpersonal support, or clear goals? When they put this question to hundreds of managers, 95 percent got it wrong.

It turns out that inner work life—positive emotions, strong internal motivation, and favorable perceptions of colleagues and the work itself—is the key to an innovative, productive, engaged, and committed workforce. In Amabile and Kramer's view, the fundamental job of managers is to create and sustain the right circumstances so that the employees' inner lives are mostly positive.

"As long as the work is meaningful, managers do not have to spend time coming up with ways to motivate people to do that work. They are much better served by removing barriers to progress and helping people experience the intrinsic satisfaction that derives from accomplishment," they say.

In *The Progress Principle*, Amabile and Kramer explain that:

- Small wins often have a surprisingly strong effect on people and performance.
- Small setbacks often have a disproportionately negative effect.
- Nourishing people's sense of progress is the key to sustaining their motivation and stimulating their innovation.

Social Innovation

If personal progress is important to individuals, there is also a growing sense that society's worst ills can be tackled only through a shared desire for progress. Increasingly, the talk is of "social innovation." Business, it is recognized, has an important role to play here, too.

Corporate social innovation embraces new ideas, processes, products, and business models that are specifically geared toward solving some type of environmental or social issue.

"It is very powerful," says Ioannis Ioannou, assistant professor of strategy and entrepreneurship at London Business School and shortlisted in the 2013 Thinkers50 Awards. "We have these acute, global challenges—climate change, lack of social cohesion, increasing social inequalities, the spread of disease, and so on—and social innovation has the potential to scale up to achieve positive environmental and social impacts. At the same time, it allows the organizations that engage in the resolution of these problems to remain profitable and to scale up these solutions even further." That's a win-win.

There are multiple drivers of social innovation. Professor Ioannou's research (along with that of researchers at Harvard Business School) seeks to help businesses better understand some of the dynamics that are at work in social innovation. In particular, his work has looked at stakeholder engagement, the adoption of longer-term time horizons, the ability to attract people whose values are aligned with the organization's, and the ability of corporations that engage in social innovation to accumulate financial as well as nonfinancial information to help ignite sometimes radical solutions.

Innovating Socially

Heather Hancock, managing partner for talent and brand at the business advisory firm Deloitte, believes that the financial crisis has led business leaders to start to rethink their role in society. "A lot of social innovation is about taking a broader view of the contribution you can make to many societal goals as well as making your business successful in the short and the long term—particularly in the long term, but it's got to have the short-term impact as well," she says. "The financial crisis has been an accelerator for social innovation at the corporate level."

Of course, changing the world (or an organization) is never easy. Ioannis Ioannou points to corporations, including Unilever, Nike, and Puma, that are actively engaged in social innovation. "We see some very bright examples that integrate this kind of innovation into their business model. They come up with their environmental profit and loss, for example. But even with those leaders who are ahead of the pack, we're far from getting to what one would define as a sustainable organization that socially innovates and is going to be around 30 or even 60 years down the road."

Heather Hancock suggests that we are at an early stage, but one where the nature of the dialogue has changed fundamentally. What was previously left unsaid is now high on the agenda.

It's about a company's willingness to engage in a different, perhaps more mature conversation with its stakeholders. So, for example, a lot of the problems we're talking about have always been thought of as the domain of governments. We have been through a system where governments commissioned private-sector organizations or apparently partnered with them. This tended to be based on the existing model. Now what we're seeing is government starting to understand it is one of the actors solving some of these challenges and definitely an actor in changing the institutional regime or the legal framework. But government is unlikely to generate the actual technical solution or the innovative, creative new service or approach that's going to work.

Both governments and companies are still feeling their way forward. Stumbles are par for the course. Ioannis Ioannou's work identifies two sets of mistakes that companies commonly make. The first is what he calls "the efficiency trap," and the second is the "ticking the boxes trap." In the efficiency trap, companies focus on waste management, energy management, recycling, and the like. These are important operational efficiency issues, but they are not sufficient to turn an organization into a sustainable company that is coming up with new ideas and social innovations. In the second trap, companies concentrate on ensuring that they are doing the right things rather than focusing on value-adding and innovative activities.

The will to overcome such traps is likely to increase. Research into the millennial generation repeatedly finds that these people expect innovation and societal impact to be highly important for businesses and their own role in business.

The stakes are unquestionably high—not only dealing with some of the world's biggest problems, but redefining the role of the corporation within society. Says Ioannis Ioannou: "We've seen the corporation over the years solving the production problem, but now the challenge through social innovation is to bring those problem-solving skills to this brand new domain of problems and to do so with the support or the synergies that come with a capitalist system." The challenge is laid down.

Cradle-to-Cradle Thinking

Alongside the rising importance of social innovation is the concept of sustainability. If you want an idea that should resonate with businesses over the next decade, one front runner could be the idea of *cradle-to-cradle*. This basically argues that our attitude toward environmentalism and sustainability has to change. At the moment, organizations are happy to be a little bit better. They feel virtuous simply because they recycle a little more, cut their energy usage, or do something similar. Cradle-to-cradle contends that our attitude to products and how we manufacture them remains rooted in the Industrial Revolution. It argues that products and services that generate ecological, social, and economic value can be created.

In their book *Cradle to Cradle*, William McDonough and Michael Braungart, an American architect and designer and a German chemist, map out the thinking behind the idea. "Today's industrial infrastructure is designed to chase economic growth," lament McDonough and Braungart. "It does so at the expense of other vital concerns, particularly human and ecological health, cultural and natural richness, and even enjoyment and delight. Except for a few generally known positive side effects, most industrial methods and materials are unintentionally depletive."

Among the examples of the idea in practice is the redesign of Ford's River Rouge facility. Ford invested in an $18 million rainwater treatment system that reputedly saved $50 million that the company would have had to spend on mechanical treatment. Ford also has a prototype car, the Model U, that is made according to cradle-to-cradle principles. Elsewhere, Nike has developed cradle-to-cradle shoes, and EDAG has developed a recyclable car.

Carpet-to-Cradle

One of the converts to the concept is the Dutch carpet manufacturer Desso and its former CEO, Stef Kranendijk. A 19-year Procter & Gamble veteran, Kranendijk is unlikely revolutionary material, but he has been championing cradle-to-cradle as a means of changing the company and getting ahead of the competition.

Kranendijk's conversion began when he watched a DVD of a documentary on the subject. Next, he read the book, then he contacted one of the authors.

> We produce a lot, and much of it ends up in landfills. For example, all the synthetic carpets in France, the United States, and the United Kingdom go to landfills. Elsewhere, they are incinerated—also not a great idea. We have two crises: the climate crisis and the raw material crisis. And that is what we have to solve. When I saw the program, I thought, "This is fantastic; this is what we should do because we produce so much volume and so much waste." Then I read the book and approached Michael Braungart. I said, "I

want my whole company cradle-to-cradle, and I will do it, but you will have to help me."

Kranendijk joined Desso as CEO in 2007 after the management team and a private equity firm bought the company from its American owner. Kranendijk and his team developed a new strategy focused on operational excellence, innovation, geographical expansion, and external communication. Among this quartet, innovation was seen as the key, and three drivers of innovation were identified: creativity, functionality, and cradle-to-cradle.

"Cradle-to-cradle is about making products from such pure materials that you can endlessly recycle them," says Stef Kranendijk. Immediately after the acquisition, he appointed a sustainability director, who investigated what Desso's sustainability initiatives had achieved over the previous decade. It had actually cut its energy consumption by 28 percent over that time. Cradle-to-cradle sought to move this to another level.

In Search of Purity

At the heart of cradle-to-cradle is the idea that ingredients can be reused to create high-quality products. Desso invested in a take-back system called Refinity. This takes back carpet tiles from offices, schools, and universities after 10 years' use. The bitumen is then sold to the road and roofing industries, and the yarn goes to one of Desso's yarn manufacturers.

Desso invested €20 million in a plant in Slovenia that takes the old, used yarn and depolymerizes it so that it can be reused. About 60 percent of all the carpet tiles that Desso sells worldwide now use 100 percent recycled yarn.

Like any idea, cradle-to-cradle comes with its own vocabulary. The Slovenian facility is an example of what is known as *upcycling*.

"The idea of cradle-to-cradle is to use very pure materials so that you can recycle them at a very high level. That's why they call it upcycling," says Stef Kranendijk.

> And that's what we try to do. Because if we make a carpet tile and after 10 years take it back, we can make yarn from the yarn again, we can make backing from the backing, but you might use this material to make a new office chair. The idea of cradle-to-cradle is that you have a kind of bank of pure raw materials going round and round.
>
> Basically, we have to go from a linear economy to a circular economy. We need to do a lot of urban mining—taking raw materials out of existing products—and the cradle-to-cradle concept fits fantastically within that. It will ensure that we only use pure materials so they can be recycled rather than toxic materials.

No Halfs

It quickly becomes clear that there can be no half measures, no half revolutions in this cyclical approach. Desso aims to have all of its products cradle-to-cradle by 2020. It also aims to be using only renewable energy by that time. It has installed 23,000 square meters of solar panels on one of its Belgian plants. It is also investing in six-megawatt wind turbines, biomass fermentation to produce biogas, and geothermal energy.

Having started with carpet tiles, Desso is now looking at artificial turf, which currently has have a latex backing, for upcycling. The company has developed hot-melt technology that ensures that the backing can be reused. Among its more ambitious innovations is to make yarn from bamboo—it has excellent antibacterial properties, apparently.

"The fantastic thing about cradle-to-cradle is that it's all about innovation. You talk all the time about design and raw materials, and focus on what end users want, corporate social responsibility, and the ultimate sustainability strategy," says Stef Kranendijk. "But it is a lot of work and costs a lot of money, because analyzing all your ingredients is hard work. It's grinding. It took us a couple of years."

With Profits

Of course, a concept without profits is an empty commercial experience. But there is a growing body of evidence suggesting that social responsibility can be profit enhancing. Research by Ioannis Ioannou at London Business School and George Serafeim of Harvard Business School, for example, has made the links between being good and doing well explicit.

"One of the most important questions regarding sustainability is its impact on financial performance. In an empirical study of two matched sets of firms covering an 18-year period, we found strong evidence that the high-sustainability firms significantly outperformed the low-sustainability firms, measured in both accounting and stock market terms," says Ioannou (who has also written a case study of Desso). "There are significant differences in corporate governance and stakeholder engagement between the two sets of firms. High-sustainability firms have a longer-term time horizon, have more long-term investors, and place a greater emphasis on measuring and reporting nonfinancial information."

A Wider Lens

What unites social innovation and the notion of personal progress is the willingness to break down the silos of the mind. Where once we might have preferred to keep society and business separate, there is now a much greater understanding that business is part of, not separate from, the broader society. Companies require a license to operate. They must demonstrate their worth to the society that they are part of.

At the same time, as the ideas in this book amply demonstrate, innovation is becoming less secretive and more open to outside influences. No company, industry, or country can afford to ignore developments outside its borders. Indeed, cross-pollination is the order of the new day.

How, then, can organizations and managers ensure that they cast their innovation nets wide? In his 2012 book *The Wide Lens: A New Strategy for Innovation,* Ron Adner offers some ideas.

Adner is a professor of strategy at the Tuck School of Business at Dartmouth College, New Hampshire, and was previously at INSEAD.

He argues that many companies fail because they focus too intently on their own innovations, while neglecting the innovation ecosystem on which their success depends. In an increasingly interdependent and global world, Adler argues, winning depends on more than simply delivering on your own promises. It means ensuring that a host of partners—an entire ecosystem, in fact—deliver on their promises, too. It is only by viewing the world through a wide lens that companies can hope to thrive in the future.

By extending that logic and widening that lens to take in people and society as a whole, innovation can be a force for good in the world, and human ingenuity can drive progress.

The Don of Innovation

Innovation, as we have seen, has made the journey from being linked narrowly with technological and mechanical progress to being more broadly defined and much more broadly ambitious. Among the very few thinkers who have also made this journey is Don Tapscott, an adjunct professor of management at the Joseph L. Rotman School of Management at the University of Toronto and one of the world's leading authorities on innovation, media, globalization, and the economic and social impact of technology on business and society.

The author or coauthor of 14 books, Tapscott wrote the 1992 bestseller *Paradigm Shift*. His 1995 hit, *The Digital Economy*, changed thinking around the world about the transformational nature of the Internet, and two years later he defined the Net Generation and the "digital divide" in *Growing Up Digital*. His 2000 work, *Digital Capital*, introduced seminal ideas like "the business web." His other books include *The Naked Corporation* (2002); *Grown Up Digital* (2009); *Wikinomics: How Mass Collaboration Changes Everything*, the bestselling management book in 2007; and *Macrowikinomics* (2011).

Tapscott is also the energy behind Global Solution Networks, a new, landmark study of the potential of global web-based networks for cooperation, problem solving, and governance. When we spoke with Don Tapscott, we asked him to begin by discussing the organization.

Can you explain the organization and its ambitions?
There are new models about how we go about solving the world's problems, cooperating, and governing ourselves on this planet, and I've undertaken a big project to research these. Just to be clear, I'm not actually going to solve the world's problems in the next two years—there's a fine line between vision and hallucination—but, essentially, our models for solving problems today came out of Bretton Woods at the end of the Second World War, when we created the World Bank and the IMF, and a little later the World Trade Organization (it was the GATT at the time) and the International Standards Organization. The G20 and so on are all institutions based on nation-states.

But increasingly, our problems are truly global, and the nation-state, while necessary, is insufficient as a vehicle for solving these problems. Meanwhile, enter the Internet and a whole bunch of other big drivers that are now causing us to examine new, more dynamic, more resilient network models of addressing problems. These are multistakeholder networks that are not controlled by states and are not based on states, but they're becoming material, and some of them are expanding and growing on an astronomical scale. We know nothing about these.

Some of these global solution networks are quite distinctive—Kony 2012, for example. Can you tell us a little bit about that?

Yes. The African warlord Joseph Kony is a bad guy. He has, allegedly, kidnapped 60,000 children; the boys become soldiers, and the girls become sex slaves. If they misbehave, he'll cut off their face or force them to kill their families. So this multistakeholder network, called Invisible Children, decided, "We're going to make Joseph Kony famous," and they created this half-hour video. When I saw it on a Monday night, 12,000 people had seen it. By Friday, more than 85 million people had seen the video.

The thing about the material is, it had a huge impact on the world, but it shows both the promise and the peril of these new networks. It's inspired, but is it legitimate? Who is it accountable to? Where does the money go? How do you determine the policy of this thing? Is it right that we should have more U.S. troops in Uganda? Is that the correct approach to Joseph Kony? What do you do when your leader has a meltdown, which occurred in this case? So it shows the yin and the yang of these new global solution networks: they can grow rapidly and virally, have great efficacy, and be impactful, but there are many, many things that we don't understand about how to make them truly effective.

It turns out that this is the classic case of the blindfolded people and the elephant. Some people think that these things look like a tree, a wall, a snake, or whatever, but there are, in fact, nine different types of networks.

I'll give you some examples. We have policy networks that develop policy for the world, but are not based on states. The International Competition Network would be an example of that. We have a second type called knowledge networks. We've had research consortia developing knowledge on a global basis before, but we've never had something like Wikipedia, TED, or knowledge networks that can be massive and have a huge impact. There are advocacy networks, like Kony 2012, that are advocating change. There are new things that I call platforms. These are now trying to solve problems—cooking fires, human rights, conflict, entrepreneurship, or whatever—by creating a platform where others can do that. There are watchdogs, like Human Rights Watch, that have hundreds of researchers out around the world identifying and documenting human rights violations. There are networks that are developing standards in the world, but they're not controlled by states the way the International Standards Organization is. We have governance networks that actually govern something on the planet.

In December 2012, there was a big battle in Dubai between the UN, the International Telecommunications Union, and the ecosystem that controls the Internet. It was an example of the old state-based models versus the new dynamic network models, and the Internet won.

Then we have what I call global network institutions. These are entities like the World Economic Forum, the Clinton Global Initiative, and Business for Social Responsibility; they're starting to look like a chunk of the UN, but they're not controlled by states. These things are having a huge impact on the world. They're engaging millions and millions of people, and they hold vast promise for helping us address the big challenges on this shrinking planet of ours.

What does this mean for nation-states? Are they now irrelevant? Have they become an inappropriate way to deal with global problems?

The nation-state is not irrelevant, and it's still appropriate in the sense that it's not going to go away. Nation-states came out of an earlier period in history where they were really part of the transition from a very intuitive society to an industrial society. Yesterday, I came back from traveling in India. India wasn't really a nation-state until 1947, and it wasn't the current nation-state until 1961, when it took over Goa from the Portuguese. Italy wasn't a nation-state until 150 years ago. And we created these national economies, generally with a common language, a sense of national identity, institutions of governance, internal policy, domestic policy, currency, and so on.

It was a good idea—nation-states for national economies—except for the little detail that, increasingly, we have a global economy. So, arguably, the nation-state and its institutions are the wrong size to address these global problems. That's one of the scope challenges of my project: it's hard to imagine a problem in the world today that can't be addressed differently.

I gave you some examples, but let's just take the case of climate change. This is a big problem. Most people agree that we have climate change, global warming, and extreme weather, and that this is largely based on human activity. So Bill Clinton says to us that if we reduce carbon by 80 percent by the year 2050, it will still take 1,000 years for the planet to cool down. In the meantime, some bad things are going to happen—you can expect a billion and a half people to lose their water supply in the next 10 or 15 years. So all these nation-states go to Copenhagen, Cancun, and Rio and try to get a deal. Not for 80 percent, but for around 6 percent, and they can't do it.

Meanwhile, there's a global solution network, a set of multistakeholder networks, involving tens of millions of people. They're not Malcolm Gladwell slacktivists who go onto Facebook and say that they're changing the world. They are people who are actually doing something. There are architects who are trying to figure out how to retrofit buildings. There are kids in schoolyards all around the world who are trying to reduce carbon in their communities. There are various policy people who are thinking about carbon credits and new ways of engaging states and solving these problems.

This is the first time in human history that the world is being mobilized and we're all on the same side. We've been mobilized before during world wars, but we were on different sides. So it is a great example of an issue that our traditional institutions are having problems with, and we're starting to see real progress with the new resilient dynamic network model.

Who else is involved?

There are a number of leading thinkers that are involved, including Vint Cerf, Tim Berners-Lee, Richard Florida, Anne-Marie Slaughter, Roger Martin, and Pankaj Ghemawat. Some of them are business thinkers, and this is a program that business is very much engaged in and should care a lot about because businesses can't succeed in a world that's failing. There are huge global business issues, like entrepreneurship, competition, regulation of the financial systems, and all kinds of issues that traditional state-based institutions are struggling with.

My goal is to get the world's leading thinkers who have an interest in and care about this issue collected in one group, and we're making some good progress.

The project is being funded, so far, primarily by corporations, and we've got some big companies that care a lot about the business issues related to this. We have financial services companies that care about global problems like cash. Cash is a global problem. It's the foundation of crime and corruption. It is obviously related to financial inclusion. Because of cash, we have trouble taxing people and funding states appropriately. So there are a whole bunch of subset issues that corporations are involved in helping us research and helping us fund.

The problems of the world will never go away. There will always be new frontiers and new challenges. But innovation in its many and hugely varied forms will always be the answer.

Notes

Introduction

1. All quotations are from author interviews unless otherwise
   noted.

Chapter 1

1. Markides, Constantinos, and Geroski, Paul, *Fast Second*, San
   Francisco: Jossey-Bass, 2005.
2. Brown, Tim, "Design Thinking," *Harvard Business Review*,
   June 2008.
3. Chesbrough, Henry, "Open Innovation," in *Financial Times
   Handbook of Management*, 3rd ed., eds. Stuart Crainer and
   Des Dearlove, Harlow, U.K.: FT/Prentice Hall, 2004.

Chapter 2

1. Bower, Joseph, and Christensen, Clay, "Disruptive Technologies: Catching the Wave," *Harvard Business Review*, January–February 1995.

Chapter 3

1. Prahalad, C. K., and Ramaswamy, Venkat, *The Future of Competition,* Boston: Harvard Business Press, 2004.
2. Ibid.
3. Ibid.
4. Ibid.

Chapter 4

1. Birkinshaw, Julian, and Crainer, Stuart, "From R&D to Connect and Develop at P&G," *Business Strategy Review*, Spring 2007.
2. Chesbrough, Henry, "Open Innovation," in *Financial Times Handbook of Management*, 3rd ed., ed. Stuart Crainer and Des Dearlove, Harlow, U.K.: FT Prentice Hall, 2004.
3. Ibid.
4. Ibid.

Chapter 6

1. Management Innovation Lab, "New Frontiers," 2010.

Chapter 8

1. Crainer, Stuart, "The Thought Leader Interview: W Chan Kim and Renee Mauborgne," *Strategy+Business*, January 2002.

Acknowledgments

We would like to thank Steve Coomber for his help with this book. We are also grateful to our Thinkers50 colleagues Joan Bigham and Deb Harrity for their essential and creative contributions. We would also like to thank all the people we have interviewed over the last 20 years writing about business thinking—in particular, Clay Christensen, Gary Hamel, Linda Hill, W. Chan Kim, Matt Kingdon, Costas Markides, Roger Martin, Renée Mauborgne, Bernd Schmitt, and Don Tapscott. We would especially like to acknowledge the intellectual generosity of the late C. K. Prahalad.

Index

About the Authors

Adjunct professors at IE Business School in Madrid, Stuart Crainer and Des Dearlove create and champion business ideas. They are the creators of Thinkers50 (www.thinkers50 .com), the original global ranking of business thought leaders. Their work in this area led *Management Today* to describe them as "market makers par excellence."

As journalists and commentators, Stuart and Des have been asking difficult questions for more than two decades. Now, they help leaders come up with their own wicked questions and explore how best to engage with people and communicate the answers. They were advisors to the 2009 British government report on employee engagement, and associates of the Management Innovation Lab at London Business School.

Their clients include Swarovski, the Department of Economic Development in Abu Dhabi, Fujitsu, and Heidrick & Struggles.

Stuart and Des have been columnists at the *Times* (London), contributing editors to the American magazine *Strategy+Business*, and edited the bestselling *Financial Times Handbook of Management*. Their books include *The Management Century*, *Gravy Training*, *The Future of Leadership*, and *Generation Entrepreneur*. These books are available in more than 20 languages.

Stuart is editor of *Business Strategy Review*. According to *Personnel Today*, he is one of the most influential figures in British people management. Des is an associate fellow of Saïd Business School at Oxford University and is the author of a bestselling study on the leadership style of Richard Branson.

Des and Stuart have taught MBA students, professors, and senior executives in programs all over the world. These include the Oxford Strategic Leadership Programme at the Saïd Business School at Oxford University; Columbia Business School in New York; the Tuck Business School at Dartmouth College in New Hampshire; IMD in Lausanne, Switzerland; and London Business School.

About the Thinkers50

The Thinkers50, the definitive global ranking of management thinkers, scans, ranks, and shares management ideas. It was the brainchild of Stuart Crainer and Des Dearlove, two business journalists, who identified a place in the market for an independent ranking of the top management thinkers. First published in 2001, the Thinkers50 has been published every two years since.

In 2011, Crainer and Dearlove added a number of award categories and hosted the first ever Thinkers50 Summit, described as "the Oscars of Management Thinking." The 2011 winner was Harvard Business School's Professor Clayton Christensen. The previous winners were C. K. Prahalad (2009 and 2007), Michael Porter (2005), and Peter Drucker (2003 and 2001).

The ranking is based on voting at the Thinkers50 website and input from a team of advisors led by Stuart Crainer and Des Dearlove. The Thinkers50 has 10 established criteria by which thinkers are evaluated:

- Originality of ideas
- Practicality of ideas
- Presentation style
- Written communication
- Loyalty of followers
- Business sense
- International outlook
- Rigor of research
- Impact of ideas
- Power to inspire

Business strategies from
THE WORLD'S MOST ELITE BUSINESS THINKERS

FEATURING
DAN PINK • ROSABETH MOSS KANTER
LYNDA GRATTON • TAMMY ERICKSON

THINKERS
50

Management

Cutting-Edge Thinking to Engage and
Motivate Your Employees for Success

STUART CRAINER + DES DEARLOVE

FEATURING
W. CHAN KIM AND RENÉE MAUBORGNE
ROGER MARTIN • C.K. PRAHALAD
RICHARD D'AVENI

THINKERS
50

Strategy

The Art and Science of
Strategy Creation and Execution

STUART CRAINER + DES DEARLOVE

FEATURING
DON TAPSCOTT • CLAY CHRISTENSEN
VIJAY GOVINDARAJAN • GARY HAMEL
LINDA HILL

THINKERS
50

Innovation

Breakthrough Thinking to Take Your
Business to the Next Level

STUART CRAINER + DES DEARLOVE

FEATURING
JIM COLLINS • WARREN BENNIS
BARBARA KELLERMAN
MARSHALL GOLDSMITH

THINKERS
50

Leadership

Organizational Success Through Leadership

STUART CRAINER + DES DEARLOVE

Available in print and eBook

Mc Graw Hill Education | Learn More. Do More.
MHPROFESSIONAL.COM

Wake Tech. Libraries
9101 Fayetteville Road
Raleigh, North Carolina 27603-5696

WAKE TECHNICAL COMMUNITY COLLEGE

3 3063 00162390 8

DATE DUE

WITHDRAWN

3/14

GAYLORD   PRINTED IN U.S.A.